The Flexibly Grouped Classroom

ASCD MEMBER BOOK

KRISTINA J. DOUBET

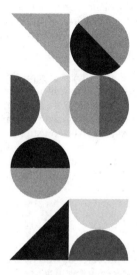

The Flexibly Grouped Classroom

How to Organize Learning for Equity and Growth

Alexandria, Virginia USA

1703 N. Beauregard St. • Alexandria, VA 22311-1714 USA
Phone: 800-933-2723 or 703-578-9600 • Fax: 703-575-5400
Website: www.ascd.org • Email: member@ascd.org
Author guidelines: www.ascd.org/write

Ranjit Sidhu, *CEO & Executive Director*; Penny Reinart, *Chief Impact Officer*; Genny Ostertag, *Managing Director, Acquisitions & Editing*; Allison Scott, *Senior Acquisitions Editor*; Julie Houtz, *Director, Book Editing*; Katie Martin, *Senior Editor*; Thomas Lytle, *Creative Director*; Donald Ely, *Art Director*; Samantha Wood and Derrick Douglass, *Graphic Designers*; Keith Demmons, *Senior Production Designer*; Kelly Marshall, *Production Manager*; Shajuan Martin, *E-Publishing Specialist*

All web links in this book are correct as of the publication date below but may have become inactive or otherwise modified since that time. If you notice a deactivated or changed link, please email books@ascd.org with the words "Link Update" in the subject line. In your message, please specify the web link, the book title, and the page number on which the link appears.

PAPERBACK ISBN: 978-1-4166-3103-3   ASCD product #121012
PDF E-BOOK ISBN: 978-1-4166-3104-0; see Books in Print for other formats.
Quantity discounts are available: email programteam@ascd.org or call 800-933-2723, ext. 5773, or 703-575-5773. For desk copies, go to www.ascd.org/deskcopy.

ASCD Member Book No. FY22-4 (Jan. 2022). ASCD Member Books mail to Premium (P), Select (S), and Institutional Plus (I+) members on this schedule: Jan, PSI+; Feb, P; Apr, PSI+; May, P; Jul, PSI+; Aug, P; Sep, PSI+; Nov, PSI+; Dec, P. For current details on membership, see www.ascd.org/membership.

Library of Congress Cataloging-in-Publication Data
Names: Doubet, Kristina, 1969- author.
Title: The flexibly grouped classroom : how to organize learning for equity and growth / Kristina J. Doubet.
Description: Alexandria, Virginia, USA : ASCD, [2022] | Includes bibliographical references and index.
Identifiers: LCCN 2021045592 (print) | LCCN 2021045593 (ebook) | ISBN 9781416631033 (Paperback) | ISBN 9781416631040 (PDF)
Subjects: LCSH: Ability grouping in education. | Team learning approach in education. | Inclusive education.
Classification: LCC LB3061 .D68 2022 (print) | LCC LB3061 (ebook) | DDC 371.2/54--dc23/eng/20211106
LC record available at https://lccn.loc.gov/2021045592
LC ebook record available at https://lccn.loc.gov/2021045593

31 30 29 28 27 26 25 24 23 22   1 2 3 4 5 6 7 8 9 10 11 12

This book is dedicated to the administrators and faculty who generously welcome me into their schools and classrooms. You and your students remain my greatest teachers.

THE FLEXIBLY GROUPED CLASSROOM

How to Organize Learning for Equity and Growth

Preface

On a bitter cold day in Chicago, my colleague, Jessica Hockett, and I met to finalize the outline of this book. Although the *idea* for the book had been rattling around in our minds and hearts for some time, it wasn't until that day in January 2020 that we finally made concrete plans for its *construction*. We parted, excited to bring it to life.

And then, the world began to unravel.

The arrival of COVID-19 upended so much of everyone's "normal," and pandemic-related complications led Jessica to the difficult decision to bow out of our book project. I found myself a solo author wondering if her topic was relevant anymore. After all, with schools shut down, students couldn't even sit in the same classroom, let alone work in an instructional group. Like many educators, the initial move to online learning sapped me of energy and passion, and I considered bowing out, too. In light of such upheaval and sorrow, I asked myself, how could I focus on writing a book about classroom grouping? What difference could it possibly make?

Then spring 2020 brought the murder of Ahmaud Abery in a "citizen's arrest," the slaying of Breonna Taylor by police in her home, and the horror of George Floyd's life being drained from him, deliberately and methodically, by a police officer's knee to his neck. The eruption of outrage and despair that followed may have been triggered by these three murders, but it was a long-brewing response to years and years of systemic racial oppression enacted through the institutions of U.S. society. School has been, and remains, one of those institutions. And for decades, decisions about how to group students for instruction have been the means of denying equitable learning opportunities to students with low socioeconomic status—especially those who are Black or Brown. In light of this disparity, this injustice, how could I *not* write a book about classroom grouping, seeing that it was a concrete way I really might make a difference?

In truth, the process of desegregating school is ongoing. When *Brown v. Board of Education* overturned *Plessy v. Ferguson*'s "separate but equal" public education policy, schools themselves *may* have become desegregated, but separation remained. Black and white students *may* have attended the same schools, but they rarely attended the same classes. In many cases, higher-level and accelerated courses were reserved for white students, while students of color were relegated to remedial classes. Further, teachers' expectations for their students generally mirrored the label or "level" of the class. Thus, while white students rose to the expectations of both their curriculum and their teachers, Black and Brown students, denied meaningful learning experiences and the expectation of growth, languished (Darling-Hammond, 1997, 2000).

This system of tracking finally came under fire in the 1980s and '90s (see Oakes, 1985, 1997; Slavin, 1996), but it has taken until the present day for many districts to commit to detracking or "deleveling" their courses. And even after detracking, the disparity between the expectations for Black and white students remains. We see evidence of this in students of color being disproportionally *over*-represented in referrals for both disciplinary action and emotional behavioral disorders and disproportionally *under*-represented in recommendations for accelerated/gifted programs and help with learning disabilities (Fish, 2017; Groeger et al., 2018). For example, a study conducted by Rachel Elizabeth Fish found that teachers "were more likely to see academic deficits in white students as 'medicalized problems to fix,' while Black and Latino students with the same deficits were seen as ordinary" (Zimmerman, 2016, para. 9).With too many teachers holding such biases, and even more teachers locked into teaching models that are not culturally responsive to their students' needs, many students of color are forced to hide their brilliance in classrooms that continue to value codification and compliance over creativity and compliance over collaboration (Emdin, 2016; Gay, 2017; Perry et al., 2003).

And so, because deleveling alone does not make classrooms equitable, we educators must shift our focus to what happens *in the classroom itself*. Teachers' decisions about instructional grouping have far-reaching implications for student success. In truth, regardless of larger district or school structures, the practices and strategies associated with classroom-level grouping have the power to build students up or tear them down, uncover gifts that students have to offer or keep those gifts under wraps. Further, the opportunity for a teacher to group equitably within the classroom is neither enhanced nor limited by how students are assigned to classes at the school level (e.g., the "level" of the course itself, such as honors, advanced placement [AP], or remedial). *Any* teacher of *any* grade or subject in *any* school can and should adopt equitable classroom-level grouping as standard practice.

Once these realizations took hold in me, writing this book became an imperative—my opportunity to join the chorus of antiracist teaching voices by speaking to what I know best: the classroom as an ecosystem in which the health and viability of all students depends heavily on how the teacher decides to leverage grouping practices. It is my hope that the guidance outlined in this book shines a spotlight on what needs to be dismantled and equips teachers with a new set of norms, strategies, and systems to do so. And, as students and teachers unite once again in face-to-face classrooms, I also hope that this book will help teachers see with fresh eyes the promise and possibility of authentic student collaboration.

Introduction: How Traditional Models of Grouping Fall Short

Everyone has real-world experiences with being grouped. Sometimes we find that the group has been chosen for us, such as a table assignment at a wedding reception, a project team at work, or college roommates. Other times, we choose our group, such as when we join a book club or Facebook group, sign up for a conference session or exercise class, or go on a guided tour. How we feel about each "grouping" depends on innumerable factors, including who else is in the group, how long the group lasts, and what the group accomplishes.

For all the groups we flow into and out of over a lifetime, school might be the place where our earliest, most formative grouping memories are etched. With little effort, most of us can conjure the joys, pressures, and pains of being in—or not in—certain school-set or school-adjacent social, academic, and extracurricular groups: feeling *included* when *invited* to a lunch table or *excluded* when *relegated* to an open seat alone; being *a part* of the Blue math group working cooperatively on complex problems or sitting *apart* in the Red math group to complete another set of rote drills; having an *affiliation* with others cast in the school play or experiencing *alienation* when we do not make the cut.

Such experiences in and with various groups shape how people see themselves and their peers. This holds especially true of *instructional grouping* within classrooms; the decisions districts, schools, and teachers make about who should be learning together and why they should be learning can really affect student performance (see Organisation for Economic Co-operation and Development [OECD], 2010, 2012; Schofield, 2010).

We know grouping matters. But how does it matter? And how much? And why? And what, exactly, does "grouping" even mean?

Classroom Portraits

The following set of classroom scenarios* will launch our exploration of these questions. These portraits illustrate how teachers tend to think about and use instructional grouping; they also reflect students' potential experiences with and feelings about the grouping approach the teacher uses. Each is followed by a few "glows" (positives to celebrate) and "grows" (areas for improvement).

Grouping Approach: Standing reading groups

Ms. Bonelli's 1st graders work in **standing reading groups** throughout the year. These groups are leveled according to diagnostic test scores and designated by colors (Blue, Green, Yellow, and Red). Although Ms. Bonellli adjusts group assignments every nine weeks to reflect the most recent diagnostic indicators of progress, many students remain with the same groupmates from the beginning of the school year until its end.

Ms. Bonelli appreciates the community students form when they work together in the same group for an extended period of time. She also values the classroom-management advantage the standing groups convey; students' color-coded groups are a shortcut for assigning other classroom activities, scheduling family presentations, coordinating field trips, and so on. At the same time, she can be frustrated by the conflicts that such familiarity breeds among students in the same group. She also wonders why more students don't make the progress they need to "move up" to a different group on a quarterly basis.

If Ms. Bonelli could see inside her students' heads, she would understand that they wish they could have more opportunities to work with classmates other than those in their standing groups. Many children have interests in common with, and prefer to learn in similar ways to, classmates who are in other groups, but the opportunities for Ms. Bonelli and her students to discover those hidden similarities are rare.

Glows: Assessment evidence is used to form and adjust groups. It is important to examine classroom data when determining appropriate instructional practices, including those around grouping.

*The teachers in these scenarios are composites. Throughout the book, I have used different naming conventions to distinguish the real teachers who have graciously shared their experience with me (identified by first and last names on first mention, and first names thereafter) from these composites (who are consistently "Ms." or "Mr.").

Grows: Students are placed in groups that reflect only a single dimension of who they are and how they learn.

Grouping Approach: Socratic seminar circles

Mr. Ross uses the **Socratic seminar** approach as the primary means of instructing his 12th grade English students. He keeps desks in a circle to facilitate these discussions, and his students (24–28 in number, depending on the section) stay in this formation during other activities, including individual work. When Mr. Ross has a substitute teacher, he allows students to work in small groups to complete the worksheets he leaves for them. The circular seating doesn't really lend itself to small-group discussion, however, so students usually end up working with a single partner—the person seated next to them. They usually work with these same partners when peer editing their writing, so it feels natural, if sometimes a little stale.

Although Mr. Ross loves Socratic seminars—he believes strongly that students should "run" class discussion—he realizes that not everyone participates equally. He uses individual writing conferences to connect with his less vocal students, but such conferences are time-consuming, and he isn't able to conduct them as often as he would like.

Mr. Ross's less vocal students look forward to individual conferencing as much as he does. They feel frozen on the large stage of the whole-class group, hesitant to share their ideas. Even students who would share ideas don't always get to do so, especially if it takes them longer to process these thoughts; someone else always seems to "jump in" before they can speak. They may be sitting in the big circle, but a lot of the time, they don't feel like a part of it.

Glows: Mr. Ross's use of Socratic seminars provides an avenue for inquiry-based learning and encourages higher-order thinking in those who participate. Further, his use of writing conferences presents him the opportunity to offer students tailored feedback.

Grows: Unless the Socratic seminar strategy is combined with additional structures and scaffolds, it can become a conversation among a small number of students— typically, those who are confident and comfortable with verbal processing (in English). In addition, the infrequency of writing conferences means Mr. Ross's students receive targeted feedback for only a small number of assignments.

Grouping Approach: Project-based learning groups

Mr. Driver's 4th grade class embraces **project-based learning** (PBL); accordingly, his students work in project groups for extended periods of time. While Mr. Driver forms these groups primarily based on students' interests or choice of project focus, he also takes each student's past academic success into consideration, being sure that each group includes students at a variety of these "levels."

While this approach lends itself to efficiency (the higher-performing students are often elected as "project managers" and take charge of project completion), it also fosters inequities in how valued students feel and in the amount of work each group member does. Further, Mr. Driver's efforts to scaffold the groups' success are complicated by the different kinds of support or challenge each group member needs; the time he spends with project groups feels inefficient.

When his students are not working in project-based groups, Mr. Driver lets them choose their own partners to complete collaborative tasks. When this occurs, some students end up working alone; frequently, it's the same students every time. Some solo workers lean into this as a release from the pressure of collaborating, but for others, working individually isn't a choice; they were edged out, perhaps because their classmates view them as being too "needy." These students wish their teacher knew that such rejection makes the crowded classroom feel like a lonely place.

Glows: Project-based learning is an approach that has been shown to be effective for students "across grade levels and racial and socioeconomic groups" (Terada, 2021). Additionally, Mr. Driver finds a way to conduct small-group instruction within this larger learning schema.

Grows: Consistent use of heterogeneous groups highlights students' status differences (academic, social, and so on), hindering collaboration both within groups and in the class as a whole. Mr. Driver misses opportunities to use small groups strategically to target students' diverse learning needs.

Grouping Approach: Cooperative learning

Ms. Williams also places her middle school pre-algebra students into heterogeneous configurations for **cooperative learning**, typically using her gradebook to form quads made up of one high achiever, one low achiever, and two students who fall somewhere in the middle. She likes that the high-achieving student in each group can serve as a peer tutor. When peer tutoring isn't enough to support learning, she pulls a group of struggling students and offers reteaching.

These middle schoolers are very aware of who consistently gets more help from their peers and from their teacher, and this is embarrassing for many of them. Ms. Williams senses this, but she reassures herself that it's "worth it"; her students' pass rate for the standardized test is almost always acceptable. What she doesn't know is that many of the students she considers to be "high achievers" grow weary of shouldering the responsibility of supporting the rest of their groupmates. These same students often feel like they can't ask questions of Ms. Williams because they are expected to know the answers. Many of them wish that they could meet more often with Ms. Williams to ask the questions they have, learn more, and go deeper. Other students in the classroom, recognizing that they are considered to be "in need of extra help" or "just average," hesitate to offer their insights and feel that if they did speak up, their voices would be ignored.

Glows: Ms. Williams's consistent use of small-group work for processing fosters opportunities for student discourse and the expectation of collaboration.

Grows: The perception of students as "high achieving," "low achieving," or "average" is inaccurate and flattens students into one-dimensional identities. No student has every answer every day; likewise, no student needs help to solve every problem. Recognizing and responding to the truth that each student possesses both areas of strength and areas for growth is an important first step to moving everyone forward in their learning—and doing so in a respectful way.

Grouping Approach: Whole-group instruction and discussion

Mr. Pfeiffer doesn't do much small-group work with his 10th grade history students. He loves history and plans his lectures fastidiously. He relies on **whole-class instruction** and **whole-class discussion** to explore any questions that arise. Mr. Pfeiffer is grateful for the students who regularly contribute to these conversations, and he reasons that their questions and responses represent what the rest of the class is thinking, feeling, and wondering.

He does pride himself on his use of the **jigsaw** strategy, which he finds to be a handy tool for breaking down long readings into more palatable chunks. It's routine for him to divide textbook chapters, primary source documents, and articles into three parts and alphabetically assign students a portion of the whole, which they later share and discuss in trios. Most students are happy to avoid reading the entire chapter, document, or article, and many find the regular opportunity to discuss complicated and complex material rewarding. But the segmented reading approach and reliance on groupmates to see the big picture limit others' understanding. Students for whom reading is a struggle often miss the important points they should share with their trios; this tends to breed misunderstanding for the other group members. Faster readers recognize this phenomenon, so they usually end up reading the whole piece themselves, anyway. They find that the repeated use of jigsaw slows them down and grow to resent their classmates who need more time to process the reading.

Glows: Use of discussion breaks up lectures and improves attention; use of jigsaw fosters collaboration.

Grows: Mr. Pfeiffer's assumption that the handful of student-questioners speaks for the full group is an inaccurate one. If he could see inside his students' heads, he would realize their responses to his lectures include confusion and boredom as well as keen interest. His use of the jigsaw strategy to engage students with readings has problematic facets, as jigsaw is best used with content and skills that represent different perspectives or facets rather than with readings or processes that are sequential in nature.

Grouping Approach: Whole-group instruction and lab partners

Down the hall, Ms. Young relies on **lab partners** as her primary means of grouping her advanced placement (AP) Biology students. She reasons that because the AP exam is an individual pursuit, her means of preparation should mirror the means of assessment. Ms. Young does enjoy circulating throughout the classroom and talking with student pairs during their lab work. Occasionally she wonders if she could replicate that phenomenon in other areas of instruction, which is typically whole-class.

And yet, the pressure of preparing for the AP exam always leads Ms. Young back to what she knows and feels comfortable with: whole-class instruction accompanied by individual practice and application. Her students are motivated and achievement driven, and so, for the most part, they comply and do well. Labs are by far their favorite part of the class, though; students feel like actual scientists during lab work—not only because of the inquiry and physical activity, but because of the opportunity it gives them to talk through their ideas and discuss scientific principles with their classmates. They wish they could do that more often.

Glows: Lab work is an authentic form of collaboration in the sciences.

Grows: Careers in science increasingly require collaboration (Bennett & Gadlin, 2012)—more collaboration than Ms. Young's students are getting. Further, research shows that students who pursue project-based learning in AP classes have a higher pass rate on AP exams than those who receive more traditional, test-prep instruction (Terada, 2021).

In each of these scenarios, teachers are using *grouping* in some fashion; however, none of these teachers uses *flexible grouping*. Because they do not group flexibly, issues such as a lack of motivation, stymied growth, and concerns about status inevitably surface—sometimes for all students in the class but almost always for certain subgroups. Holding on to what works (the "glows") and changing what does not work (the "grows") in each grouping scenario above would go a long way toward helping each individual student make substantial strides in the social, emotional, and intellectual realms of their being. This, in turn, would foster a healthier sense of community and collaboration.

About This Book

This book explores how teachers can capitalize on the possibilities that flexible grouping affords us and our students. In the coming chapters, you'll find guidance, examples, and tools that will help you

- Better understand the purpose and benefits of flexible grouping.
- Plan for more effective flexible grouping.
- Implement a progression of flexible grouping.
- Acquire a variety of practical procedures for flexible grouping.
- Address potential pitfalls of flexible grouping.
- Embrace the full promise of flexible grouping.

This book also includes a set of Appendixes with a planning template, two sample grouping plans (one for the elementary grades and one for middle or high school), and a list of online resources (links to videos, blogs, articles, etc.) to help clarify how the informed use of flexible grouping can positively transform classroom practice.

As you reflect on the guidance in this book, I hope you will see that the success of flexible grouping depends in large part on the successful combination of many little tweaks to familiar community-building and instructional routines. Such transformation may take a semester or a year to implement, but the time invested is worth it. When a teacher and students work together as a team to embrace flexible grouping, the gains in equity and in intellectual, social, and emotional development can be significant and exhilarating. As the African proverb advises, "If you want to go fast, go alone. If you want to go far, go together."

Let's spend some time examining how to go far together.

1

The Purpose of Flexible Grouping

Flexibly grouped classrooms are necessary both because the world is changing and because it has not changed enough.

Adapting to the Modern Workplace

As dependence on technology grows, more and more routine jobs (such as factory work) have become automated. Remaining and emerging occupations require employees to have social and collaborative skills that cannot be replicated by technology (Deming, 2017; National Association of Colleges and Employers [NACE], 2018).

Collaborative group work has indeed become ubiquitous in the modern workplace, both in face-to-face and online environments. In fact, "the time spent by managers and employees in collaborative activities has ballooned by 50 percent or more" since the mid-1990s (Cross et al., 2016, p. 74). This changing world of work is driven in part by studies showing that "groups tend to innovate faster, see mistakes more quickly and find better solutions to problems" than individuals do (Duhigg, 2016, para. 12).

Recognizing this increase in collaboration, Google (2016) conducted an internal study to determine the defining qualities of an ideal team—one whose members planned, made decisions, and reviewed progress in a highly collaborative, interdependent manner. Codenamed "Project Aristotle," the study concluded that successful teams share the following characteristics:

1. *Psychological safety.* Team members feel safe to take risks and be vulnerable in front of one another.
2. *Dependability.* Team members get things done on time and meet a high bar for excellence.
3. *Structure and clarity.* Team members have clear roles, plans, and goals.

4. *Meaning.* Team members find the work they are doing personally meaningful.

5. *Impact.* Team members think the work they are doing matters and creates change.

Note that these characteristics reflect *principles* rather than *logistics*. In other words, they reflect the *health of team relationships* and the *nature of the team's work*—not the traits of individual team members.

Other studies of the emerging workplace reinforce the value of employees being socially nimble—that is, being able to effectively communicate and collaborate with a variety of people (NACE, 2018). Deming (2017) notes that "the fastest growing cognitive occupations—managers, teachers, nurses and therapists, physicians, lawyers, even economists—all require significant interpersonal interaction" with a diverse range of individuals (p. 1595).

If school is to meet the changing demands of the workplace, it must help students learn to effectively exercise social skills and to grow in their collaborative capacities. Fortunately, such a shift aligns with what we know about how people learn. Echoing Project Aristotle's findings, educational research reveals that student growth depends in large part on two principles: (1) *a healthy classroom environment* (Hattie, 2012; National Academies of Sciences, Engineering, and Medicine [NASEM], 2018), and (2) *meaningful, relevant, and engaging curriculum and instruction* (McTighe & Willis, 2019; NASEM, 2018). Research also affirms the belief that students should have the opportunity to interact with a wide range of classmates in both low- and high-stakes settings. Fluid movement in and out of instructional groups provides this opportunity and helps to build "intellectual camaraderie," a hallmark of a healthy classroom community (Bransford et al., 2000; NASEM, 2018).

Opposing a Stagnant System

While the world of work has changed before our eyes, within schools, there are many deep-seated systems reinforcing division and inequity that have not changed nearly enough. Instructional grouping is one of those systems.

Instructional grouping can refer to everything from how students are assigned to classrooms, specialized services and programs, and leveled (tracked) courses to how teachers organize students for instruction within the classroom. I am a staunch advocate for dismantling tracking at the district and school levels, as research from all parts of the world confirms that tracking hinders the growth of the vast majority of students (see OECD, 2012). However, tackling such a large-level change lies beyond the scope of this book. What this book can and will address is reforming the kind of instructional grouping that occurs at the classroom level.

Teachers make decisions every day about how to use groups in their classrooms, even if they choose to rely solely on whole-group instruction or individual work. While studies have shown that group work in general has a positive effect on student achievement (see Lou et al., 1996), not all group work has the same impact. When decisions about instructional grouping are based on a single factor and remain static, group work tends to hinder student growth, erode classroom community, exacerbate status differences, and reinforce the racial, cultural, and socioeconomic inequities present in our larger society (Batruch et al., 2019; Hattie, 2009; OECD, 2012). On the other hand, when decisions about instructional grouping are based on a variety of student learning needs and ensure that students change groups frequently and purposefully, group work can foster growth, provide access to equitable learning experiences, strengthen student capacity for collaboration, combat status differences, and build empathy. This dynamic approach to grouping at the classroom level is called *flexible grouping*.

What Is Flexible Grouping?

Essentially, flexible grouping is a system of organizing students intentionally and fluidly for different learning experiences within a classroom over a relatively short period of time. The groupings are *flexible* because they align with specific, changing goals, and because decisions about group size, membership, and longevity are guided by recent classroom assessment results or other student or class characteristics that are relevant to a specific instructional purpose.

Flexible grouping is not a formula or a set of steps, but there are several "hallmarks" of flexibly grouped classrooms. These are principles that, when applied together, make and keep flexible grouping "flexible."

Hallmark 1: Groupings change based on goals and student characteristics that matter for the task

When grouping is flexible, the teacher employs a range of grouping configurations that depend on and change with instructional goals and tasks. Too often, when a teacher claims to use flexible grouping, it means that groups change only *if and when* the teacher sees a need for change. In practice, this might mean students need to "prove themselves" to the teacher in order to be "released" from a static grouping, or that the teacher is letting intuition and personal comfort—or even the manageability of group size—guide the decision to change a grouping (Jean, 2016).

Flexible grouping assumes that groupings *will* and *must* change, because students' readiness needs, motivations, and learning preferences routinely change.

Hallmark 2: Groupings vary in composition, duration, and size

Just as a hand mixer won't fry an egg and a pair of tongs can't ladle soup, no single grouping system can meet all instructional needs. The Introduction's example scenarios included several established grouping configurations, including standing reading groups, project-based learning, cooperative learning, lab partners, whole-group instruction, and Socratic seminar circles. While there is a time and a place for each of these approaches, none of them can serve *every* instructional purpose.

There are times when groups of three or four work best (e.g., to facilitate creative brainstorming) and other times when partner work is more efficient (e.g., to provide direct one-on-one feedback). Heterogeneous groups may be optimal for test preparation, but homogeneous groups are preferable for targeted instruction, especially when they are composed based on recent classroom-level assessment evidence. Project-based learning groups may engage in sustained inquiry together, but teachers can form smaller, more temporary groups of students (pulled from each project group) to "catch up" students who have been absent, to coach individuals to be technology "experts," or to peer edit and rehearse interview questions.

Hallmark 3: Students consistently work with a range of peers

Grouping isn't flexible if students make sense of ideas, discuss content, practice skills, or create products with the same classmates, day in and day out. While group work isn't the only setting in which students develop relationships with one another at school, it is a chief mechanism for bringing them together in the classroom. There is no hard and fast rule for how often group composition must change, but over the course of a few weeks, students should have opportunities to interact with most, if not all, of their classmates in the service of purposeful discussion or tasks. Carol Ann Tomlinson (2005) put it this way: "After a month's time, every student should have had the opportunity to both *be challenged* and to *be the challenger*." A good "test" for whether students are consistently working with a range of peers is to periodically ask them to make a list of their classmates' first and last names and provide facts about each (an interest, a favorite musical artist, a hobby). The results are a fairly dependable barometer of how flexible the groupings in the class really are.

It's important to note that flexible grouping is a means to an end, rather than the end itself. The act of forming or being in *any* kind of a group won't "save" poorly designed instruction. Although peer collaboration can provide opportunities to facilitate growth (see Vygotsky, 1978), poorly designed collaborations can *deny* students that access just as easily as grant it (Jean, 2016; Lou et al., 1996). In other words, both groups and group tasks need to be carefully and strategically planned in order for students to benefit from group work.

How Does Flexible Grouping Intersect with Differentiation?

Flexible grouping is a hallmark of a differentiated classroom. In Tomlinson's model of differentiation, flexible grouping refers to the practice of planning "a consistent flow of varied student groupings within a unit of study based on the nature of the work and the individual needs of students" (Tomlinson & Imbeau, 2010, p. 90). Many grouping configurations (e.g., like-interest, like-readiness) can function as delivery systems for differentiated tasks. It's important to note, however, that groups can also be a means of increasing instructional efficiency, building community, resetting attention, increasing motivation, and so on. Said differently, flexible grouping *facilitates differentiation*, but it serves other purposes as well. We will examine the relationship between flexible grouping and differentiation more closely at the end of this book.

Why Group Flexibly?

Flexible grouping combats the power of school to establish, reinforce, and justify stereotypes by granting learning privileges to some and denying them to others. Such inequities flow from various school structures, most notably tracking—the practice of sorting students into levels that they stay in throughout much of their school experience.

Tracking remains a prominent structure in today's schools, despite both decades-old and more recent evidence outlining the dangerous inequities it promotes (Batruch et al., 2018; OECD, 2012). In tracked (or "leveled" or "streamed") systems, students are sorted into different "ability pathways" for their schooling, with some students pursuing "advanced" levels and others remaining in "general" or even "remedial" classes. Decisions about which track students will be assigned to are usually based on standardized test scores that reflect a student's status at one moment in time and ignore the influences of social, cultural, emotional, economic, and experiential (e.g., trauma) factors on learning. They reflect blanket assumptions about the potential of students based on limited evidence and "condemn" students with "less ability" to coursework that is less rigorous, less relevant, less authentic, and less engaging, often for the remainder of their school career.

Teachers in tracked classrooms sometimes internalize and reinforce the stereotypes dictated by designated levels (Kelly & Carbonaro, 2012), *but this does not have to be the case.* Even in leveled classrooms, teachers who incorporate flexible grouping can shake up both their own expectations of students and their students' expectations for themselves and their peers by consistently changing the lens through which they view student performance. When students flow in and out of groups based on like interest, like need, and preferred ways of taking in or demonstrating knowledge, student affinities for the curriculum—and for one another—bubble to the surface. Flexible grouping can, among other things, showcase students' learning *strengths* rather than deficits, and it can do so regardless of students' perceived "levels" at initial placement.

Thankfully, some schools and districts have heeded the warnings about tracking and have begun to move from tracked classes at the middle and secondary levels (see Burris & Welner, 2005; Tomlinson et al., 2008). These districts and schools may collapse three or four levels of some subjects into two levels or even one. But shifting students into more heterogeneous settings is just that—changing their setting, and providing students with "new geography" is not enough to advance equity. Gallagher (1997) reminds us that the real work is attending to what is happing to students in their changed setting. Teachers not trained for this newfound diversity may gravitate to systems that functionally *hide* student diversity (e.g., whole-class instruction), *exploit* it (e.g., cooperative learning), or *fixate* on it (e.g., ability grouping or creating smaller "tracks" within a classroom). No matter the grade level, none of these fixed structures actually *harnesses* the power of diversity. That is what flexible grouping can do.

Flexible grouping capitalizes on the rich tapestry of talents present in any classroom, giving students equal access to important learning experiences and, in turn, cultivating growth, building classroom camaraderie, strengthening students' collaborative capacity, combating status differences, increasing exposure to diverse perspectives, and fostering empathy. Let's take a closer look at each of those benefits.

Benefit 1: Flexible grouping grants access to equitable learning opportunities

In a flexibly grouped classroom, students work with a variety of their peers in different configurations to achieve multiple purposes. In classes with static groupings (e.g., Ms. Bonelli's 1st grade class from the Introduction), students are often "retracked" within the class by perceived ability, most often for reading instruction. When this kind of grouping structure is the only one used, some students consistently receive remediation and lower-level tasks (Sparks, 2018). If, however, a variety of groups are used—groups based on interests, learning preferences, and other factors as well as on academic readiness—these same students have the opportunity to shine in other areas.

In one study of emergent talent at the primary level, students remained in their established reading groups but were "regrouped" for other subjects (including math) based on the results of frequently administered classroom assessments. "Wendall," a student in the lowest reading group, surprised his teacher when formative assessment data indicated he should be in the most advanced group for certain measurement tasks. His teacher reflected, "Wendall kind of surprised me when we were reading the book *How Big Is a Foot?* because he's not the one to participate as often as the others, but he was the first one to come out with the response we were looking for. Wendall was up with the high group, which he usually is not" (Brighton, 2007). Not only did the use of flexible grouping grant Wendall access to the more challenging task, but it also provided him a setting in which he could thrive. This helped him grow in both his competence and confidence. This is the promise of a flexibly grouped classroom.

Benefit 2: Flexible grouping cultivates growth

As illustrated in Hallmark 2's "kitchen tools" metaphor, in no single grouping structure cultivates growth in every scenario. Elizabeth Cohen's (1998) work on complex instruction advocates for the creation of groups made up of *students with different talents*, all of which are needed to complete a complex task. This model holds promise for project-based learning; if the project is complex enough, multiple skills will be needed to achieve success. Determining the diverse skills necessary for task completion can lead to the formation of groups wherein every student can play to his or her strengths (McTighe, 2020).

On the other hand, some learning goals are best met with students working in *like-readiness groups*, because this setting is an efficient way to for provide proper tools and tasks to students in small-group settings (Hattie, 2012). Gifted students, in particular, seem to benefit from such opportunities to work with likeable peers (Steenbergen-Hu et al., 2016). At other times, it makes the most sense for students to work in *like-interest groups*, because motivation in shared interests drives investment, persistence, and, in turn, increased learning (Dabrowski & Marshall, 2018). Finally, temporary groups made up of students who have *chosen the same way to complete a task* (e.g., analytical, creative, or practical) can facilitate the efficient processing of information (Sternberg & Grigorenko, 2007). In a flexibly grouped classroom, students are afforded each of these opportunities, with different groupings used for different purposes, all with the goal of fostering growth in each student.

Benefit 3: Flexible grouping builds classroom camaraderie

"Simply put, emotion drives attention, and attention drives learning," asserts neuroscientist David Sousa (Ferlazzo, 2017, para. 13). He also cautions that classroom environments are not neutral; students feel either positively or negatively about being there (Sousa & Tomlinson, 2018).

To be sure, students have good and bad experiences in a class for many reasons that are beyond the teacher's control. But much of what happens in the classroom *is* within the teacher's power to shape or influence, including building a sense of community among students. Students may or may not sit together at lunch, connect on the playground, or follow one another on social media, but inside the four walls where they learn math or history, they share more than just oxygen. When teachers (1) establish safety and norms, (2) build trust with students, and (3) facilitate the positive interactions among a variety of classmates, they build a classroom camaraderie that fuels positive emotions and sets the stage for powerful learning experiences (Bransford et al., 2000; Sousa & Tomlinson, 2018).

Benefit 4: Flexible grouping strengthens capacity for collaboration

The camaraderie just described does more than facilitate learning in the classroom; it prepares students for the highly collaborative world of work they will someday enter. Recall the discussion of the increasing demand for a socially skilled workforce at the beginning of this chapter. When students become accustomed to working with a variety of classmates toward shared goals in an atmosphere of safety and productivity, they are more likely to successfully replicate those conditions in other situations, be it next year's classroom or a future workplace. In other words, flexible grouping doesn't just prepare students for the collaborative future; it also prepares them to be *leaders* in that future.

Benefit 5: Flexible grouping combats status differences

Teachers' grouping decisions send powerful messages to students about their roles in and value to the classroom community. When they are put into a group, most students "size up" the learning situation, thinking, *Who's in my group? Who's in that group? What are we doing? What are they doing?* In essence, they are conducting a kind of "status check," trying to detect clues about what the teacher believes about their abilities.

Flexible grouping fights the development of classroom hierarchies and makes it difficult for students to pigeonhole one another or themselves. Although groups are sometimes based on students' readiness or skill level, these are interspersed with groupings based on interest, learning preference, experience, and other factors. In classrooms where flexible grouping is a way of life, students stop fixating about who is in each group and what that means, because they know that groups will change soon.

Benefit 6: Flexible grouping exposes students to varied and divergent perspectives

Children are no different from adults in the way that they gravitate toward people who share their points of view, have similar experiences and interests, and seem to value the same things. Wanting to stick with friends or familiar classmates is normal and sometimes helpful. But students can also get too comfortable or stuck in a rut when they work with the same peers, day in and day out.

Flexible grouping pushes students out of their comfort zones and into interactions with peers they might not otherwise choose or get a chance to learn from. These interactions very often lead them to discover shared experiences and interests. Perhaps more significant, they lead to a better understanding of appreciation for what makes each classmate unique. Flexible grouping gives students the chance to see the world through more of their peers' eyes, affording them a view they might not otherwise gain and wider perspective on life.

Benefit 7: Flexible grouping fosters empathy

Martin Luther King Jr. (1956) taught us that to live in this new world, "we must rise above the narrow confines of our individualistic concerns, with a broader concern for all humanity." That kind of living starts in the classroom. It is never too early for students to begin reaching beyond their own feelings to try to understand the feelings of others—in other words, to strive for empathy. This means not only seeing things from another's perspective but also, as Brené Brown explains, being willing to jump into the pit with them, if necessary (RSA, 2013). Such understanding, love, and compassion are needed in our world now more than ever before.

● ◼ ✖

In the chapters ahead, we will examine practical strategies for both planning and implementing flexible grouping, and discuss how to anticipate and avoid potential grouping pitfalls. We will also explore frequently asked questions about flexible grouping and return to the classroom scenarios from the Introduction to see how "upgraded" grouping practices play out in a variety of grade levels and subject areas.

A final note of emphasis: While flexible grouping is ideal for highly diverse classrooms, it can be used in *any* classroom to accomplish the aims described in this chapter. Even in classes where it seems that all students are the same due to ascribed level, shared linguistic needs, advanced placement, or choice of elective, differences do exist. Flexible grouping makes it possible to capitalize on the excitement of diversity that occurs in *any* setting where more than one person is present.

2

Planning for Flexible Grouping

Successful grouping stems from a thoughtfully planned approach that both anticipates and responds to students' needs.

Think again of the various grouping scenarios common to everyday life: a table assignment at a wedding reception, a project team at work, a book club, an exercise class, and so on. How well any of these groups—or any group at all—functions depends on a variety of factors that should be carefully contemplated by the one who does the grouping. For example, when a couple plans seating assignments for their wedding reception, they usually consider whether guests know and like each other, and, if they do not, what they might have in common (age, vocation, hobbies, etc.). When a boss forms a project team, she may try to unite individuals with varied strengths, compatible temperaments, or a common cause. And when people "self-group"—join a club or sign up for a class or volunteer project, for example—they are usually driven by a shared interest or goal.

Factors to Consider When Forming Instructional Groups

Decisions about grouping in the classroom follow a similar process, with the teacher considering the *goal or purpose* of grouping, the *duration of the group arrangement,* each group's *composition* and *size,* the *characteristics of students* in each group and *who will be responsible for forming the group.* Let's examine each of these grouping factors in more detail. For a bird's-eye view of the six factors, see Figure 2.1 on page 25.

Factor 1: Use or purpose of grouping

While the other factors can be addressed in any order, it's vital to begin with purpose. The first question to ask is *"What educational purpose will grouping serve right now?"* The answer will drive decisions about the other grouping factors. It's also important to note that if there *isn't* an answer to that question, it's OK to decide not to use groups for a task. In other words, teachers shouldn't group simply for the sake of grouping.

Group work can serve many functions, both general and specific. One of the simplest and most common purposes of grouping is *to build community.* Ms. Ball, a kindergarten teacher, forms "dance party quads" at the beginning of each school year to help her young learners connect to one another and give them a safe and fun way to let off steam. Dance quad formations change each week, and the leaders—who get to make up the dances—rotate each day. Bonds build among students as they work out their wiggles. Similarly, high school English teacher Katie Carson frequently "mixes up" her students into teams to complete short, nonacademic challenges such as seeing who can construct the tallest tower out of bits of paper and paper clips. According to Katie, these challenges are a way to celebrate students who might not be celebrated academically and foster the understanding that everyone in the class is an expert at something, and everyone's contributions are needed for a group to succeed (Tomlinson & Doubet, 2005).

Perhaps the most frequent reason teachers use group work is to infuse efficiency and support into academic tasks. Collaboration is a great way for students *to practice or apply skills,* such as critical thinking skills and skills of a discipline, and *to process new ideas.* Such shared rehearsal constitutes the "You do it together" phase of the gradual release of responsibility model (Fisher & Frey, 2021) and helps students make sense of and solidify their grasp of complex ideas in the company of peers. Group work is also a way for students to *investigate new content,* particularly if they will be able to access that content via a variety of different media. Similarly, teachers often find it useful for students *to examine a text, primary source, or data set* in pairs or groups, as more than one set of eyes facilitates careful investigation. Likewise, a classmate's "second set of eyes," offered during peer review, can catch blind spots in a student's work and provide valuable feedback, especially when used in combination with success criteria (McTighe et al., 2020). Finally, group work is a way *to engage in project-based learning* (PBL) aimed at solving complex, real-world problems (Larmer et al., 2015).

Factor 2: Group duration

The purpose of the group and the goals it's designed to meet will determine how long the group will remain active. The key question to ask when determining a group's duration is *"How long will it take for this group to achieve its purpose?"*

If the group is formed to build community or reinforce general collaborative skills, the group will most likely stay together for *less than a class period.* If the group is set up to practice a discrete skill or refamiliarize students with a skill they have used before, that group may also last less than a class period. On the other hand, if the group is formed to practice new or complex skills in context or to explore lengthy sources and data sets, that group may need to stay together for *an entire class period or even two.* If a group is investigating a truly complex problem, group work may consume *the majority of the week* but be flanked by a full-class launch at the beginning and a whole-group share at the end. Finally, if students are completing a multifaceted PBL assignment, their collaboration will most likely extend *beyond a week,* although it's important to note that students can temporarily move out of their project groups to work in any of the other kinds of academic configurations discussed under Factor 1 (e.g., focused skills practice, source examination) in the pursuit of individual growth and project completion. In this case, the PBL group would stay standing for the duration of the project, but students would move fluidly in and out of more temporary grouping configurations as needed.

Factors 3 and 4: Student characteristics and group composition

Because Factors 3 and 4 work hand in hand, they are best addressed together. The key questions for both are *"What student characteristics matter for this task or learning experience?"* and *"Should the groups constructed with these characteristics in mind be homogeneous or heterogeneous?"*

A good place to start is with the set of student variables identified by Carol Ann Tomlinson (2014): readiness levels, interests, and learning preferences. *Readiness* refers to a student's "entry point relative to particular knowledge understanding or skills" (p. 18). A student's readiness changes from topic to topic and skill to skill, and it is revealed by the ongoing use of formative assessment. Such frequent learning checks reveal, for example, whether a student is "ready" to analyze a complex graph without scaffolding or if they need guiding questions or highlighting to support their examination. *Interest* refers to a "learner's affinity, curiosity, or passion for a particular topic or skill" (p. 19). All students have personal interests they bring with them into the classroom (e.g., pets, video games, crafting, superheroes, sports, music) as well as interests they discover during the course of instruction (e.g., a species of animal, the poetry of Langston Hughes, the process of creating a proof, a particular historical figure). Students also enter the classroom with different *learning preferences*, meaning the ways in which they are most comfortable learning: by reading text versus listening to it, by explaining a concept with verbal analogies versus straightforward descriptions or diagrams, by demonstrating understanding through writing versus illustrating, and so on. A student's learning preferences are not set in stone; they can vary and shift over time, much as readiness and interests do.

And, of course, students also vary in more *personal ways*, such as cultural background, ability to empathize, or willingness to take charge. These, too, are valuable considerations when thinking about how to set up groups.

With the purpose of the grouping in mind (Factor 1), identify which set or sets of student characteristics would best support this purpose, and then decide more specifically how the group should be composed: *homogeneously*, with all group members sharing the targeted characteristics, or *heterogeneously*, with group members representing a range of those characteristics. For example, are students in different places in their mastery of a certain skill (e.g., reading complex text, solving equations, conducting experiments)? If so, then it makes sense to set up *like-readiness* groups and give each group tasks that target members' particular areas of strength or weakness. Does the lesson topic need more "spice"? Perhaps placing students in groups of *similar interest* to explore the topic through that "lens" will increase their motivation and engagement. Following this initial exploration, putting these students into *mixed-interest* groups would be a way to let them share their findings and explore the topic in more breadth. Students' partialities for accessing content (e.g., reading about it, watching a video about it) can be a way to form *like-learning preference* groups.

Heterogeneous groups work well when a mixture of perspectives and backgrounds—including experiences, beliefs, leadership styles, extracurricular endeavors—is important. This is why, when forming PBL groups, it is usually a good idea to unite students around common topic interests but to make sure there are a variety of other characteristics (e.g., readiness levels, interpersonal skills) represented in each group. For example, students investigating the environmental impacts of natural disasters may work in groups with others who chose the same event, but within each of those like-event groups, there is at least one student who excels in data analysis, another who thrives in making real-world connections, another with the gift of empathy, and another who is an effective communicator.

Factor 5: Configuration/size

The fifth factor to consider is group size. As with Factors 1–4, think first about how the size of the group would best support the group purpose while still keeping efficiency mind. The key question associated with Factor 5 is *"What size makes the most sense, given the learning activity's goals and our particular circumstances?"*

For example, *groups of four* serve as an ideal setting for collaborative analysis and problem solving. *Groups of five* can also work well for this purpose, but there is a subtle reduction in the efficiency of production as group size increases. On the other hand, the richness of a discussion is enhanced by the variety of perspectives present in larger groups. For this reason, *circles of six to eight* tend to produce more robust discussions than do smaller groups.

If students are not accustomed to working in groups, it's a good idea to begin with *partners* or *trios*. Working in these smaller groups helps students get used to both speaking and listening in a social context and keeps them from being overwhelmed by a chorus of voices. Partners and trios are also ideal for students learning English, as it gives them a relatively safe and contained space to practice using their new language skills (Ferlazzo & Sypnieski, 2012). As students grow more comfortable and skilled working with peers, you can expand the sizes of their groups.

Finally, a *split-class configuration*—dividing students into two large discussion groups, "fishbowl" style (i.e., the inside circle talks, the outside circle listens, and then the groups switch; see p. 94)—is a good choice when the goal is to harness the power of diverse viewpoints and contribute to a livelier discussion. The split-class configuration also works well for test review and debate coaching, especially in a co-teaching context.

Factor 6: Formation determination

The final key grouping question to consider is *"Who will determine the grouping formations?"*

Often the answer to this question is the teacher, and understandably so. After all, it's the teacher who is best positioned to gather student assessment data, diagnose what each student needs to grow toward mastery, and prescribe the task and grouping configuration that will best address those needs. The teacher is also best positioned to collect information on student interests and assign students to like-interest groups; this approach ensures that students actually work in an area of interest with peers who share that interest (rather than just feigning an interest in order to work with their friends). Luckily, when students work in shared-interest groups, they often form new friendships.

There are times when it makes sense for students to form groups—to choose their own partners and trios—and it's usually for low-stakes tasks of short duration. When using this formation approach, be sure to keep a close eye on the class to make sure no one is left out. "Compass partners"— described on page 37— provides one structure to ensure students always have a partner in student-choice groupings.

We can also let "chance" determine groups through a variety of mix-it-up strategies (which we will discuss in detail in Chapter 3). These *random groupings* keep things fresh and help ensure that students work with the widest possible array of peers.

Figure 2.1 features an overview of the decisions involved in purposeful group planning. While this figure is well-suited to guide decisions about specific groupings for particular assignments, setting up a flexibly grouped classroom means going further. It requires us to "zoom out" for a broader consideration of how different types of grouping arrangements can be used together and in succession to pursue more complex instructional goals.

The Factors in Action: Planning a Flexibly Grouped Unit

Let's take a look, then, at two classrooms in which teachers facilitate multiple grouping configurations for different purposes to form flexibly grouped units.

An Elementary Classroom

Justin Minkel, a teacher at Jones Elementary School, in Springdale, Arkansas, flexibly groups his 1st grade students across subjects throughout the school day and over the course of several months.

Figure 2.1

An Overview of Purposeful Planning: Six Factors to Consider

Factors	Options
1. Use or Purpose of Grouping *What learning experience has prompted the decision to group?*	☐ Building community ☐ Practicing/applying skills; processing ideas ☐ Investigating new content ☐ Examining a text, data set, etc. ☐ Peer review/feedback ☐ Working on a project
2. Duration *How long will this grouping last?*	☐ Less than one class period ☐ A class period or two ☐ Less than a week ☐ More than a week
3. Student Characteristics *What characteristics matter for this task or learning experience?*	☐ Readiness/skill level ☐ Interest ☐ Learning/thinking preference ☐ Personal gifts/backgrounds/experiences
4. Composition *Should the group be similar or mixed by student characteristic?*	☐ Homogeneous/like ☐ Heterogeneous/mixed
5. Configuration/Size *What is the best configuration for this learning activity? What size makes sense, given the goals?*	☐ Partners ☐ Trios ☐ Small groups of 4-5 ☐ Circles of 6-8 ☐ Split class
6. Formation *Who will determine group formations?*	☐ Teacher choice ☐ Student choice ☐ "Chance"/randomly

Justin uses several grouping configurations within each math unit. For example, he launches a unit on arrays with a whole-group minilesson, explaining that students will be helping a candy company make a box designed to hold a certain number of chocolates (represented by tiles). He previews the task by asking student volunteers to "fishbowl"-model (1) a version of the task and (2) norms for peer interactions. Then Justin uses the results from a pre-assessment given earlier that week to form like-readiness pairs who will build arrays using the number of tiles he assigns; the number is adjusted to provide appropriate support or challenge to each pair. To conclude, the class reconvenes to examine one another's work and discuss their findings.

In science, Justin's students work in small, like-interest groups of two or three that have chosen the same animal (e.g., cheetah, elephant, horse) for structured research. Eventually, each student will create their own "All About My Animal" book. In these animal research groups, classmates share print and electronic resources, compare their findings, and meet periodically with Justin to report progress and ask questions.

In addition to traditional reading groups, Justin uses several other kinds of reading groups in language arts that change monthly or bi-monthly. These include "fluency friends" (five to six students with similar fluency skills) and "book clubs" (right now, three to four students who chose the same book from a library of a single author's various works). He incorporates strategy circles of varied sizes and compositions to deliver more targeted instruction around skills like making inferences or sequencing. In Justin's classroom, writing groups are flexible, too. Whether students work with a buddy to give feedback, share ideas, or do a word sort, Justin uses a combination of teacher and student choice to pair and re-pair peers. Students work with such a wide variety of peers that changing groups is the norm rather than a special event. Figure 2.2 provides a snapshot of the different grouping configurations Justin employs in his classroom.

A Middle School Classroom

Before beginning her unit on *To Kill a Mockingbird*, Ms. Dawkins sought information from her 8th grade students about their interests and their readiness.

First, she used a survey to gauge their interest in some of the important background knowledge they would need to fully appreciate the novel's intricacies. Based on their responses, she formed like-interest groups to study (1) Jim

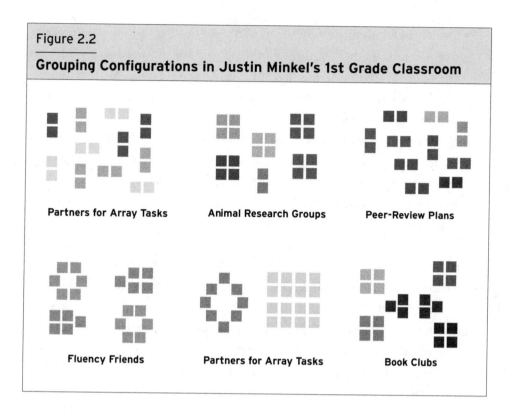

Figure 2.2

Grouping Configurations in Justin Minkel's 1st Grade Classroom

Partners for Array Tasks   Animal Research Groups   Peer-Review Plans

Fluency Friends   Partners for Array Tasks   Book Clubs

Crow laws in Alabama and surrounding states at the time the novel was set, (2) poems and stories by Black authors written during this time period, and (3) the intersection of Harper Lee's hometown (Monroeville, Alabama) and the events described in Bryan Stevenson's book *Just Mercy* and its film adaptation. After a period of research and discussion, students met in teacher-created mixed-choice groups to share what they had learned and note areas of overlap.

With the historical context and background knowledge established, Ms. Dawkins administered a pre-assessment designed to clarify students' readiness to make inferences based on implied exposition in a text. She then formed groups based on students' sophistication with this skill and assigned perspectives—or reading lenses—accordingly (Dobbertin & Doubet, 2005):

- Students who demonstrated they were ready to glean insights from abstract text read the novel through the lens of "The Outsider," Boo Radley. Although Boo is described throughout the story, he does not actually appear until the very end. The Outsider lens led students to extract Boo's perspective on people, places, and events without direct evidence.

- Students who demonstrated they were ready to make "right there" inferences examined the text through the perspective of "The Insider," Atticus Finch, or "The Wise," Calpurnia. These students were tasked with examining characters' words and actions to determine the underlying meaning behind what they *were*—and *were not*—saying and doing.
- Students who demonstrated that they needed support in making inferences examined the text through the perspective of "The Child," Scout. Ms. Dawkins's prompts consistently drew them back to questions like "Does Scout really understand what's going on here? Why or why not?" and "What does Scout understand that the adults do not?"

Students regularly met in these *like-lens* pairs and groups to discuss insights revealed by their character's focus as well as the connections they could make with the story's historical context. To keep the groups flexible, Ms. Dawkins also assigned students to various configurations of *pooled perspective* (mixed-readiness) groups to examine conflicts and events from the vantage points of different characters. *Mixed quads* met for close analysis of key scenes, while *discussion circles* of six gathered to discuss the book's overarching motifs and themes along with their connections to other texts such as current events articles, poems, speeches, and other informational texts (these like- and pooled-perspective groups are illustrated in Figure 2.3). In order to ensure groupings remained "fresh," Ms. Dawkins made it a point to use *random* and *you choose* groupings (see p. 41) at least once a week to complete low-stakes (ungraded) practice tasks focused on vocabulary, the rules of dialogue, and so on.

To finish the novel study, Ms. Dawkins divided the class in half to engage in a structured academic controversy over the statement "Things have [or have not] changed in the South since the time in which *To Kill a Mockingbird* was set." Students emerged from the novel study with a deeper understanding of history, social justice, the text—and of one another's gifts and talents.

A Valuable Tool

The reproducible Flexible Grouping Planner that you can find in Appendix A is a helpful tool for anyone who designs units of study. An expansion of the decision-making guide in Figure 2.1, this planner prompts a unit designer to (1) consider the ideal grouping for a particular task and (2) utilize a variety

Figure 2.3

Grouping Configurations in Ms. Dawkins's 12th Grade English Classroom

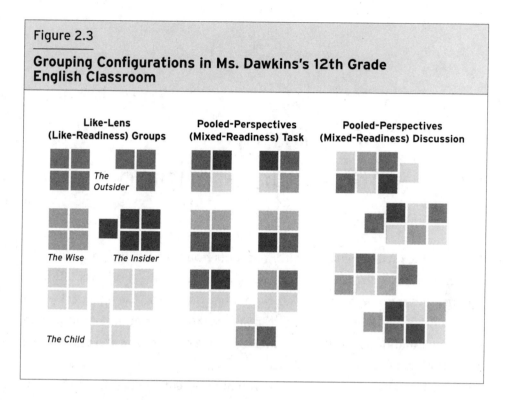

of grouping configurations within each unit. In other words, the Flexible Grouping Planner is a tool that facilitates the planning of purposeful *and* flexible grouping. The full grouping plans that Justin Minkel used are included as Appendix B; and a grouping plan for Ms. Dawkins's *To Kill a Mockingbird* unit is shown in Appendix C. A digital version of the Flexible Grouping Planner is accessible via one of the links in Appendix D.

● ◼ ✖

In the next chapter, we will move beyond "planning on the page" and begin to examine the nuts and bolts of implementing flexible grouping in the classroom and in online learning contexts.

3

The Progression
of Flexible Grouping

We ended the previous chapter with snapshots from two flexibly grouped class-rooms. Both teachers were experienced, and—as a result—both were fluid in their use and management of flexible grouping. Such expertise doesn't develop in a day, a week, a month, or even a year. Rather, it results from a commitment to growth, to building a repertoire of grouping strategies over time, and to including students in that journey toward expertise.

This chapter will provide a process, with multiple entry points, for implement-ing a system of flexible grouping in any classroom. We'll look at "the five stages of group work"—along with representative group-based instructional strategies for each stage—that progress from the simplest to design and execute to the most complex.

It's important to stress right at the outset that a teacher's goal is not to "advance" from one stage to the next but to *accumulate* strategies from each stage into a *growing collection* of grouping practices. As you read this chapter, consider (1) where *you* are in your journey toward having a flexibly grouped classroom and (2) your *students'* experience with group work. Acknowledging your own comfort level with grouping is important for goal setting; trying to do too much too quickly can hinder rather than foster growth. Likewise, students—especially those who are not used to working with peers in collaborative settings—will need to be eased into the process. The goal of this chapter is to clarify the progression of group work and familiarize you with a number of grouping strategies within each stage, so that you can determine, for yourself and your students, the appropriate next steps toward a flexibly grouped classroom.

Stage 1: "Proximity Partner" Strategies

This stage represents a first step away from whole-group instruction. It involves getting students accustomed to talking and thinking with their peers without having to get up and move or be assigned to a group. Stage 1 strategies can be implemented regardless of setting (a large auditorium, a church service, a fund-raising banquet) and with little disruption or discomfort. They include *turn and talk, elbow/rug partner discussions, think-pair-share, think-pair-square,* and *second-set partners.*

Turn and Talk

Brief and not necessarily planned, a *turn and talk* provides the opportunity for students to process information with, voice opinions to, or ask questions of a classmate or classmates sitting in close proximity. The teacher poses a question, and students turn to a peer or peers nearby (pairs or trios work best) to share responses. Turn and talks work well for "resetting" attention, brainstorming ideas, providing a "brain break," or jump-starting a large-group discussion.

Elbow/Rug Partner Discussions

Although they are used in a similar fashion to turn and talks, *elbow/rug partner discussions* occur within standing partnerships established by systems like seating charts. Because students converse consistently with the same peers, they are able to build trust and adapt to each other's speaking and listening styles. Such established partnerships are beneficial when the teacher wants to avoid "tricky" pairings that may occur when students are seated near friends or classmates with whom they have issues. Still, it's a good idea to change the seating chart every so often so that students have the opportunity converse with a variety of peers over the course of a month or a grading period.

Think-Pair-Share

In essence, a *think-pair-share* is a planned turn and talk or elbow/rug partner discussion. It is used in conjunction with open-ended questions or problems, and it provides established time for individual students to formulate an answer or work through a problem (*think*) before getting with a partner to talk about their respective conclusions (*pair*) and, ultimately, reporting their joint conclusion, often informed and enhanced by each other's perspective, to a larger group (*share*). The think-pair-share process must be taught and rehearsed to establish the expectation for both partners to share, listen, ask clarifying questions, provide feedback, and reach consensus.

Accountability in a think-pair-share is established in two ways: as the teacher circulates and listens in on pairs' conversations, and in the share phase, when students communicate their conclusions with the full class. In theory, any student can be called on to share with the rest of the class, as each has been given the opportunity to process the question both individually and collaboratively. They can even share a question developed in the pair phase rather than an individual answer. Many teachers use "share sticks" (a random draw of popsicle sticks featuring students' names) to call on students in the final stage. This adds to the feeling of accountability while infusing an element of chance to counter any sense of teacher favoritism (real or perceived) during the share stage.

Think-Pair-Square/Second-Set Partners

As the names imply, these strategies add (or substitute) a step to a think-pair-share. In a *think-pair-square*, initial pairs join nearby pairs to form quads; in this new setting, each pair shares their respective answers, asks probing questions, and provides feedback. In *second-set partners*, used by kindergarten teacher Elizabeth Iwaszewicz to support her English language learners, students follow their initial pair discussions with a "re-partner" step (Teaching Channel, 2017). In this step, each student partners with a different classmate and shares the conclusions reached in the initial think/pair. Second-set partners are encouraged to use their first partners' names in their second-set discussions in order to honor their ideas and to build community. (See Appendix D for a link to a video of Ms. Iwaszewicz using this strategy.) Both strategies can use the quad or "second set" as the concluding discussion *or* follow up with a full-class share.

Stage 1's Proximity Partners strategies "grease the wheels" of grouping, management-wise. The speaking and listening skills students develop in this stage will continue to serve them well as they advance to more complex group arrangements.

Stage 2: "Get Moving" Strategies

Once students are comfortable engaging in discussion with those in their vicinity, they can be challenged to transfer those skills to partnerships and groups formed with peers around the room. These groups are determined by chance rather than by proximity, meaning that they fall into the "random" system of group formation (the last factor in Figure 2.1).

As the stage's name implies, this category of instructional strategies gets students used to (1) physically moving into groups, (2) working in a variety of configurations, and (3) conceiving of groups as detached from any particular status or specific meaning. Stage 2 strategies include *line up/fold the line, card deck groups, grid groups and pairs,* and *compass partners.*

Line Up/Fold the Line

In the versatile *line up* and *fold the line* partnering strategies, students line up according to a teacher- or student-generated criterion—either something objective (e.g., height, birthday, time it takes them to get to school) or something subjective (e.g., how much they like chocolate, how many toppings they like on their pizza). The order of the line-up determines which students will be partnered for the upcoming activity. It might be the person they are standing next to in the line or the person standing across from them once the line is "folded," or doubled-back on itself. For a more detailed description of this strategy, see Figure 3.1.

Card Deck Groups

The *card deck groups* strategy provides several different grouping possibilities within a single class period. Here's how it works.

Before class, using a regular deck of playing cards, the teacher selects as many cards as there are students in the class, taking care to include an even distribution of numbers and suits. For example, if there are 24 students in the class, the teacher might pull the ace through the six cards for each of the four suits (club, diamond, heart, spade). Each student receives a card upon entering the classroom; alternatively, cards can be placed on students' desks before they enter, an approach that gives the teacher a bit more control over who works with whom while maintaining the appearance of random placement.

Figure 3.1

Line Up/Fold the Line

Directions:
1. Ask all students in the class to line up across the front of the room in a designated order, according to a factor such as

    - Height (e.g., shortest to tallest).
    - Birthday (month and day only).
    - Favorite color or color students are wearing (in order of ROY G BIV).
    - Distance students travel to get to school (in minutes or miles).
    - Degrees of preference for a given food or TV show.
    - Phone number (e.g., numerical order of last four digits).

2. Allow students to talk to one another as they order themselves, or increase the challenge by asking that they use only nonverbal means of communication.

3. Put a time limit on student movement to communicate a sense of urgency.

4. Once the line is formed, "fold" it in half by bringing the two ends together. Then ask students to pair up with the person across from them. If there is an uneven number, ask the middle three students to work together.

Variations:

- Once the line is formed, students can go in order and state the reason for their placement (e.g., when their birthday is, how much they love or hate the TV show).

- After you've used the strategy once or twice, keep students on their toes by varying whether they "fold" the line or pair with an odd/even partner.

Source: From Differentiation in the Middle and High School: Strategies to Engage and Equip All Learners (p. 267), by K. J. Doubet and J. A. Hockett, 2015, ASCD. Copyright 2015 by ASCD.

When it's time for students to form groups, they can assemble by like numbers, like colors, or like suits. In our 24-student example, a teacher who seeks to form quads would instruct students to meet with others who have the same card number. Similarly, partner groups could be created by calling for all same-number red cards and same-number black cards to pair up, or groups of six for discussion circles could be set up by asking students to meet with others who have a card of the same suit. Card deck groups offer an efficient way to break up a long instruction block in different grouping configurations and ensure students collaborate throughout the entire class period.

Grid Pairs and Groups

Although the teacher provides the mechanism for *grid pairs and groups*, the grouping itself is implemented solely by students, making this technique more student-directed than the others in Stage 2.

The teacher furnishes each student with a copy of a grid preprinted with the names of everyone in the class—one name per square with blank spaces below each name (see Figure 3.2). When the teacher asks the students to form grid pairs, everyone finds a partner and writes the day's date on the first blank below their partner's name, documenting their pairing. The next time students are asked to move into grid pairs, each finds a new classmate to partner with and records that day's date under that partner's name. Unless absolutely necessary, students should partner with a new classmate each time grid pairs are called until they have paired with everyone in the class; after that, they can use the second blank below each classmate's name and so on. *Grid groups* can be formed by combining two grid pairs and holding the general expectation that students will try to mix up those quads as much as possible.

It's a good idea to physically adhere students' grids to the inside of their interactive notebooks or school agendas to make sure the grids are always available and ready to use.

Compass Partners

Also known as "clock partners" (or "genre partners," "shape partners," and so on), *compass partners* is a proactive grouping structure that combines student choice and teacher choice.

Using the content area as the guide, the teacher creates a sheet with four directions (or times, genres, shapes, and so on) and leaves a space next to each for a student's name (see Figure 3.3). The teacher chooses two partners for each student (e.g., their "East" and "West" partners), and students choose two partners of their own (e.g., their "North" and "South" partners).

The teacher can be strategic in assigning partners, striving for like- or mixed-pairs according to background, experience, or personal strengths or areas for growth. When students choose their partners, they usually (and naturally) choose their friends, so it's very important for the teacher to be vigilant during this selection process to ensure that no one is left out.

Figure 3.2

Grid Pairs and Groups—Sample Template

Directions: Record the date of when you meet with each colleague.

Adriana	Asia	Andrew	DaNae	D'Shawn
Date: _____	Date: _____	Date: _____	Date: _____	Date: _____
Date: _____	Date: _____	Date: _____	Date: _____	Date: _____
Heath	**Jalen**	**Joshua**	**Mandie**	**Matthew A.**
Date: _____	Date: _____	Date: _____	Date: _____	Date: _____
Date: _____	Date: _____	Date: _____	Date: _____	Date: _____
Matt H.	**Mikayla**	**Natalia**	**Nick**	**Noah**
Date: _____	Date: _____	Date: _____	Date: _____	Date: _____
Date: _____	Date: _____	Date: _____	Date: _____	Date: _____
Pedro	**Rachael**	**Rhyan**	**Riya**	**Sarah**
Date: _____	Date: _____	Date: _____	Date: _____	Date: _____
Date: _____	Date: _____	Date: _____	Date: _____	Date: _____
Seth	**Sophie**	**Tori**	**Tyler**	**Zoya**
Date: _____	Date: _____	Date: _____	Date: _____	Date: _____
Date: _____	Date: _____	Date: _____	Date: _____	Date: _____

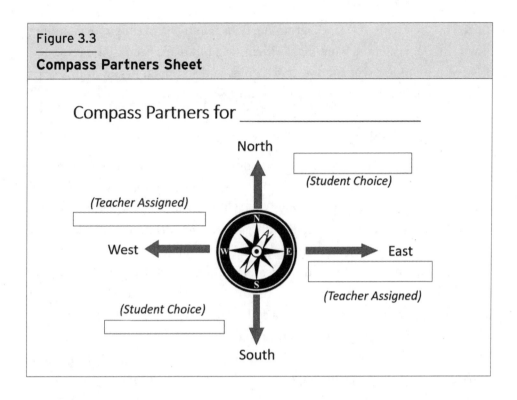

Figure 3.3

Compass Partners Sheet

Compass Partners for _____

North

(Student Choice)

(Teacher Assigned)

West ← → East

(Teacher Assigned)

(Student Choice)

South

The beauty of **Stage 2's Get Moving strategies** is that they need not—and should not—be left behind as you move into the more strategic formations in the later stages. While they are important early on for helping both students and the teacher bolster their comfort with and skill in collaborative interaction, they remain valuable until the very last day of school as a means of building community, "shaking things up," and incorporating a little movement into the classroom.

Stage 3: "We Agree" Strategies

We know that appealing to student interests is a powerful motivator (Sousa & Tomlinson, 2018). Uniting students around shared interests is a way to amplify that motivational power further.

Stage 3 strategies connect students to one another—not by chance but by similar interests or preferences that may or may not be closely tied to the learning task. As such, these techniques require a bit of planning on the teacher's part, but it need not be extensive. Stage 3 grouping does require an overall understanding of who students are and what makes them tick, but plans can also be informed by beginning-of-the-year surveys, quick polls, and so on. Strategies in this stage include *Would you rather?*, *table topics*, and *four corners.*

Would You Rather?

This strategy uses binary-response questions to break the class into two groups. The teacher poses a question such as "Would you rather eat pizza for every meal *or* never eat pizza again?" and students report to the side of the room that represents their response; there is no middle ground (literally or figuratively). Once assembled in two big groups, students break into pairs or trios to discuss their answers. When time is called, both sides share their thinking about the question (and sometimes debate ensues); then, the teacher instructs students to sit in their like-choice pairs or trios to complete a collaborative task. With the ice broken by a low-stakes discussion, students can get right to work.

In Appendix D, you'll find a link to a storehouse of *Would you rather?* questions. Some are silly ("Would you rather have to eat every meal using only a fork [no spoon] *or* only a spoon [no fork]?"), some are thought-provoking ("Would you rather be an amazing painter *or* a brilliant mathematician?"), and some are designed to tease out student reasoning ("Would you rather be able to read minds *or* teleport?"). When the strategy has become familiar, students tend to contribute their own questions.

Table Topics

The results from "getting to know you" student surveys administered at the beginning of the year can help teachers create all kinds of interest-based grouping configurations. For example, patterns in students' responses to the survey shown in Figure 3.4 might lead a teacher to form "Favorite Snack" groups, "Movie Clubs," "Gaming" groups, "Dream Vacation" groups, "Birth Order" groups (like and mixed), and "Walk-Up Song" groups (the latter asks students to share what "theme song" should introduce them as they walk onto a stage, a sports field/court, and so on).

The *table topics* technique calls for the following to be posted as students enter the classroom: group names, each group's assigned members, and a corresponding table (or desk cluster) number. When students move to their assigned tables, they first share why they chose those favorites as an ice breaker before launching into an academic collaborative task.

It's a good idea to use this strategy at the beginning of the school year because it (1) is an encouragement to genuinely scrutinize students' survey responses instead of simply filing them, (2) builds trust by showing students their teacher is paying attention to their expressed interests, and (3) helps students get to know one another and discover unexpected connections.

Four Corners

In the tried-and-true *four corners* cooperative learning strategy, each classroom's four corners is designated with one of four interest-oriented choices—anything from favorite movie genre (comedy, romance, action, sci-fi) to favorite milkshake from McDonald's (vanilla, chocolate, strawberry, or shamrock) to best thing about the weekend (sleeping in, catching up on shows, spending time with friends/family, playing sports). Students head to the corner that represents their choice and gather in pairs, trios, or quads to discuss their answers. After that initial greeting, they find a place to sit and begin the posted collaborative task.

As the examples in the preceding paragraph illustrate, the corner choice need not have anything to do with the task students will undertake: it can simply be a mechanism for forming random groups. However, it is possible to correlate the corner choices with the actual work to be completed. For example, the corners could represent four topics of high interest to students (e.g., sports, fashion, video games, and phones). When students arrive at their corner, they might find advertisements related to their chosen topic to analyze for persuasive techniques or story problems (featuring the same data set, numbers, operations, etc.) written to relate to their topic. Linking corner choice to content takes slightly more planning (i.e., finding different ads, adjusting context of story problems) than using the technique purely as a randomization mechanism. It's fair to say that the content-linked application of four corners dips a toe into Stage 4.

 The goal of **Stage 3's We Agree strategies** is to help students connect with a wide variety of classmates over shared interests that are easy and fun to talk about. Although they are well suited to beginning-of-the-year community building, Stage 3 grouping can be used whenever teachers want to infuse variety, movement, and interaction into their lessons. In addition, because Stage 3 strategies direct students to

Figure 3.4

Student Survey

Your Name:

What you like about your name, where it came from, or someone who shares it:

Favorite snack:

Favorite movie or show:

Favorite game (video, board, card, etc.):

Where you would like to travel someday:

Your "walk-up" song (and why):

Your "age order" among your siblings (check all that apply):

☐ Only
☐ Oldest
☐ Youngest
☐ Middle
☐ Other (explain if you want to)

Explain, if you'd like:

Areas of strength:

Areas for growth

Design a personal logo (explain its meaning on the back of this sheet).

On the back of this sheet, please explain at least one more thing that you'd like me to know about you.

general locations (sides of the room, table numbers, corners), they prepare students for movement into more *task-specific locations* in Stages 4 and 5.

Stage 4: "You Choose" Strategies

Stage 4 grouping also unites students around shared interests, but the process is a bit more nuanced. In Stage 4 activities, students make choices based on interest in—or a preference for—a *specific task* among several options. Grouping in this stage takes more planning, because students choose from teacher-created task options designed in such a way that each choice addresses the same learning goals. (A good validity check for uniform learning goals is to make sure all task options could be evaluated using the same rubric.)

Stage 4 activities don't necessarily have to be carried out entirely in groups, although they can be. For example, students might begin work independently (as a "group of one") and then gather for a few minutes with like-choice peers to check progress and augment their products based on peer feedback. After these exchanges, they might regroup to share their products in a new mixed-choice group. Remember, the goal is not simply to move students as much as possible; it's also to create the learning arrangements best suited for helping students meet your instructional goals.

The strategies in this stage celebrate diversity of thinking while reinforcing important learning goals. Stage 4 strategies include *jigsaw, RAFT,* and *TriMind.*

Jigsaw

In the popular cooperative learning strategy *jigsaw*, each member of a small group becomes an expert on a different aspect of the content and then shares this expertise with other group members.

Students begin the jigsaw process by meeting in "home groups" for task introduction and division of labor. Each home group member selects one "piece" of the larger task "puzzle" (e.g., a perspective or a subtopic). Students reconfigure themselves into "expert groups" composed of those who share the same "puzzle piece," where they work to compile information on their chosen perspective or subtopic. The teacher provides guiding questions, resources, graphic organizers, and any other necessary supports to facilitate the process. At an announced point, expert groups disband, and all members return to their home groups.

Back in home groups, each member shares their respective piece of the "puzzle," providing information, examples, and insights. A teacher-supplied graphic organizer can facilitate this sharing process. When all home group members have finished sharing, students engage in whole-class discussion to address questions, seeming contradictions, and interesting observations (Doubet & Hockett, 2015, 2017).

Figure 3.5 illustrates what a jigsaw process would look like for an investigation of abolitionists' writings. This example illustrates the importance of the teacher checking in with each of the expert groups to ensure accuracy, using a graphic organizer during the home-group share, and embedding a synthesis task in the wrap-up (closure) step to both check understanding *and* infuse accountability.

Used properly, jigsaw can motivate students, increase their sense of investment, and help the teacher address a large amount of material in an efficient manner. It can also be superimposed on other strategies; for example, you can jigsaw reading roles in book clubs or socioeconomic or political perspectives in social studies. Jigsaw is also a possible sharing mechanism for RAFT and TriMind assignments.

RAFT

The *RAFT* strategy presents students with choices for writing (formally or informally) across the curriculum, asking them to assume a *role* and consider their *audience* while working in a *format* and examining a *topic* from their chosen perspective. The teacher designs several horizontal "strips," or Role-Audience-Format-Topic combinations that become task options for students to select (Doubet & Hockett, 2015, 2017). Figures 3.6 and 3.7 illustrate a lower-grades science example and a middle grades ELA example. As you see in Figure 3.7, a teacher can present a RAFT that keeps some of the variables constant and provides choice in the others.

The amount of student choice in a RAFT can also be varied by asking students to choose among one of the set combinations ("Pick a row") or, when the grid is designed to allow for it, permitting them to mix and match roles, audiences, formats, and topics, so long as their custom combination makes sense and is aligned with the learning goals (see Figure 3.8). After a student has chosen a task (or role, if using the mix-and-match method), the teacher can distribute more detailed directions, if necessary.

Figure 3.5

Civil Rights Activists Jigsaw

Guiding Questions: How did civil rights activists in the 1950s and '60s fight for equal rights? What did they overcome? What did they accomplish?

Home groups	• Students receive images and documents on the following topics: **Freedom Riders, the August 1963 March on Washington for Jobs and Freedom,** *Brown v. Board of Education,* **and the Voting Rights Act of 1965.*** • Students decide who will be the "expert" on the activists associated with each topic. *Note: If resources are at different levels of accessibility, the teacher may choose to assign experts.* • Teacher previews the home group's synthesis task so students understand the purpose of the jigsaw.
Expert groups	• Students read and analyze the images and documents about the topics chosen (or assigned) in home groups. • Students highlight important ideas and record the **challenges** their activists faced, the **action steps** they took, and what the activists **accomplished.** • Teacher checks student answers to gauge (1) grasp of big ideas and (2) accuracy of details, redirecting as needed.
Home group sharing	• Experts return to their respective home groups; each expert shares their findings. • Home group members use a teacher-provided organizer to record their classmates' ideas and information. • After all experts present, home group members look for *patterns* emerging for all activists (regarding their **challenges, action steps,** and **accomplishments).**
Synthesis task	• Each home group creates a civil rights infographic (using a tool like Piktochart.com) depicting the hallmarks of civil rights activists' **challenges, actions,** and **accomplishments.** • Group will also examine/make **connections** to how these hallmarks are seen in civil rights activism today. • Possible roles for group members include *information organizer, layout designer, connector,* and *fact-checker.*
Wrap-up	• Each home group shares its infographic with the whole class (teacher can designate a role as spokesperson). • Spokesperson explains the group's findings along with the connections they found to modern-day activism. • Each student completes an individual reflection on the most important thing they learned and why it matters.

*Images and documents for these topics can be found at https://www.learningforjustice.org/classroom-resources/texts (free account).

Figure 3.6

Fourth Grade Science RAFT

Role	Audience	Format	Topic
Heat energy	3rd grade students	Poster or infographic	Watch my "moves" with water . . . and how I heat the cold and cool the heat!
Light energy	Planet Earth	Video	You should be grateful for me and my relationship with the sun! Here's why. . . .
Electrical energy	The wind and a wind turbine	Letter or email	I know you two are friends, but did you know you create me? Here's how. . . .

Aligned to NGSS 4-PS3-2

Figure 3.7

Middle School Grammar RAFT

Role	Audience	Format	Topic
Semicolon	Comma and conjunction	*Choose One:* • Blog post • Series of Facebook posts • Series of "pop-up" or webpage-sponsored ads	"The two of you are needy; I don't need anyone but me."
Comma	Conjunction	No matter which format you choose, your response must use all three methods for fixing a run-on sentence.	"Please come back! I can't do my sentence separation job without you!"
Semicolon, comma, and conjunction	Teens on their screens		"I'm the best for the job!"

Figure 3.8			
Economics "Incentives" RAFT			
Role (Choose One)	**Audience**	**Format** (Choose One)	**Topic** (Choose One)
Consumers	Your fellow consumers, producers, workers, savers, or investors	Letter or email	Did you see what they're offering? We can't pass that up! Here's why. . . .
Producers		Group chat	Did you see what they're offering? There's got to be a catch. Here's why. . . .
Workers		Video message	Did you see what they're offering? Is it a good deal or a bad deal? Let's see. . . .
Savers		Poster or infographic	Did you see what they're offering? It seems too risky to me. Here's why. . . .
Investors		Voicemail	Did you see what they're offering? No way. Here's what we need and why. . . .

Students can work independently on their tasks or in groups with others who choose the same (or a similar) task option. Teachers can also jigsaw the RAFT assignment and have students share their work with classmates who chose different tasks.

TriMind

The *TriMind* strategy (Doubet & Hockett, 2015, 2017) operationalizes cognitive psychologist Robert Sternberg's triarchic theory of intelligence, which posits that the human intellect is made up of three sets of abilities: analytical, practical, and creative (Sternberg & Grigorenko, 2007):

- *Analytical:* The ability to analyze, compare/contrast, see the parts and the whole, examine cause and effect, and think in linear and logical-sequential ways. Analytical abilities are the kind that are measured on most standardized tests. Think: *Bruce Banner (not Hulk).*
- *Practical:* The ability to put ideas into action, apply knowledge and skills to the real world, execute tasks efficiently, organize and motivate people, and engage in on-the-spot problem solving. Think: *Steve Rogers/Captain America.*
- *Creative:* The ability to imagine possibilities, think outside the box, innovate, invent, dream, ask insightful questions, propose novel solutions, or intuit. Think: *Tony Stark/Iron Man.*

While all human beings possess analytical, practical, and creative abilities, as individuals, we may be stronger in one than the others, especially when we are young. The TriMind strategy uses these three thinking preferences as a framework for instructional and assessment task choices.

When designing TriMind tasks, teachers generate three tasks—all aligned with the same learning goals—that appeal to creative, practical, and analytical thinking. They then present those tasks as options to students (see Figures 3.9 and 3.10).

Because we know that these intelligence preferences are fluid and change depending on a variety of factors (e.g., comfort with the material, nature of other work recently completed), it's a good idea to let students choose their preference rather than to "diagnose" them and assign tasks accordingly. It's also a good idea to present the options as "Tasks 1, 2, and 3" rather than with their labels so that students will choose the *option* that appeals to them, rather than the *label*.

Like RAFT assignments, students can work with classmates who chose the same task or work independently before pairing or grouping with like-task peers to share and provide feedback. As illustrated by Figure 3.10, mixed-choice sharing works well as a prelude to full-group closure.

Figure 3.9

Middle School Math TriMind Activity

Directions: Choose the way you want to show that multiplying integers is repeated addition.

Task 1 (Analytical)	Task 2 (Practical)	Task 3 (Creative)
Explain why multiplying $4 \times$ -3 is the same as -3 + -3 + -3 + -3.	Explain a real-world situation using $4 \times$ -3 instead of -3 + -3 + -3 + -3.	Create a new model/picture to demonstrate that $4 \times$ -3 is -3 + -3 + -3 + -3.
Sample Student Response:	*Sample Student Response:*	*Sample Student Response:*
If you jump back -3 on a number line, and you do that 4 times you end up at -12. If you make 4 groups of -3 chips you have -12 chips total.	*Mrs. Hydroflask is in debt to the water company $12 and she wants to make payments of $3 (-3) until she is out of debt (-12). She will have to make 4 payments of $3 (-3) to get out of debt, which is the same as 4 × -3.*	*(Instead, I'm doing 4 × -300 = -1200): Each hour, a sub descended 300 feet. What was the sub's depth after 4 hours if they started at the surface?* -300 + -300 + -300 + -300 = -1200

Source: Tabatha Myers, Kate Syms, and Denika Gum, 6th Grade Math Team, Lakeside Middle School, Albemarle County, Virginia. Used with permission.

Figure 3.10

World Geography TriMind Activity

Introduction

You are a highly sought-after city planning professional. You have been tasked with **designing the optimal city to encourage both local and global connections to trade.** You must be strategic in your choices, as each will play a role in whether or not your city will be a leader in world trade. Make sure to **consider geographic characteristics** that provide advantages when engaging in local and global trade. You may choose between three tasks listed below, but all tasks require you to include the information discussed in class.

Task 1 (Analytical)	Task 2 (Practical)	Task 3 (Creative)
Write a petition to send to the government officials of your home country convincing them that a new city should be built to serve as a trading hub for the nation. Include in your letter justification for your choice of the city's location.	City officials have asked you to create an implementation plan for a new city that breaks down the reasoning behind your proposed location. Create a short slide presentation that explains the factors you considered when choosing your location.	City officials have asked you to create a comic strip to be published in the local paper that will convince a new community that a new city needs to be developed to encourage trade. These officials want to generate as much business as possible, but they need you to explain to the public why the location was chosen.

Closure Activity

1. Meet with classmates who chose the same task. Discuss the location of the city and make a "master" chart of the factors discussed by group members.

2. Meet with classmates who chose a different task and add factors you identified to their master chart.

3. As a whole class, we will compare lists and discuss the Top 3 factors that were most important when choosing a location and why.

Source: Laura VanDemark, Skyline Middle School, Harrisonburg, Virginia. Used with permission.

Each of the **Stage 4's You Choose strategies** provides multiple ways of grouping students. Because each involves critical thinking, it's a good idea to build in some individual thinking or planning time before moving students into groups. Stage 4 strategies, then, provide up to four different working formations: individual (thinking and planning), like-choice (revising and fine-tuning), mixed-choice (sharing), and full-group (closure). More important, each of these formations facilitates success with different facets of the task. That's a lot of instructional "bang for the buck"! Finally, Stage 4 strategies serve as "talent scouts"; they spotlight students working in an area of shared choice or strength and collaborating with (1) others who share that choice or strength and (2) those with different, complementary strengths. This affords both teacher and students a clear view of the value of each person's contribution.

Stage 5: "Formative Formations" Strategies

This stage contains the grouping configurations most commonly associated with differentiation. Because it involves creating pairs/groups based on the most recent evidence of student grasp of a few, specific learning goals, Stage 5 groupings are fluid and change over time. The strategies in Stage 5 are mostly teacher-selected, but they can also be student-selected with guidance. Included in these strategies are *team huddles, self-assessment groups, like-pattern groups,* and *learning stations.*

Team Huddles

A *team huddle* is a classroom norm established by the teacher with the goal of removing the stigma that sometimes surrounds working in a teacher-led group—the perception that the only reason anyone would work with the teacher in a small group is to receive remediation. Implemented correctly, team huddles makes this instructional arrangement just another part of the classroom's everyday rhythm.

Team huddles respond to the needs of small groups of students (based on formative assessment, observation, and so on) and usually take place while the rest of the class is working independently, in project groups, or in stations. Teachers might call team huddles to

• "Catch up" students who were absent.

- Answer an exit-card question raised by only a handful of students.
- Clarify a misconception revealed in an assignment or assessment.
- Provide "next-level" questions for students who are ready to explore a topic in more depth.
- Provide resources to students with a specialized curiosity around a topic.
- Provide a more intimate setting for students learning English to practice their language skills.

When team huddles are used for such a variety of reasons, the huddle functions as more of a reward rather than a punishment. Fairfax County (Va.) Public School teacher Emily Knupp regularly uses team huddles in her project-based middle school science class (personal communication, June 30, 2021). She refers to these groups as her "by invitation only" groups (she also runs interest-based small groups that are "open invitation"). Team huddles not only give Emily a better way to target students' learning needs but also bring together students who normally work in different project groups; this, in turn, builds community.

Self-Assessment Groups

Middle school teacher Shawna Moore (Teaching Channel, 2018) forms team huddles based on student self-assessment. These guided *self-assessment groups* provide opportunities for differentiated levels of support (see the link in Appendix D).

The class period begins with a minilesson, after which students reflect on their understanding of the new content or skill and self-assess their readiness to complete the assigned follow-up task. The process then unfolds as follows:

1. When prompted, students designate themselves as an "A" if they need to hear the information again or hear it explained in a different way, a "B" if they understand for the most part but have a few clarifying questions, and a "C" if they are ready to complete the task without any additional direction or support.
2. When released from the minilesson, the "C" students move to the back of the room to begin work independently and quietly; the "A" and "B" students move to the front of the room into a huddle with the teacher.
3. The team huddle begins with Ms. Moore asking the "B" students to share their clarifying questions. As she answers their questions and the proverbial lightbulbs go on, students change their status from "B" to

"C" and move to the back of the room to begin work on the task. Often, these clarifying discussions turn the lightbulbs on for students who had assessed themselves as an "A." Ms. Moore has seen many of them change their status to "C" and leave the huddle to begin independent work in the designated area.

Movement out of the huddle is completely student-driven. When only "A" students remain, Ms. Moore repeats the minilesson, using different examples, clarifications, and so on until all students "get it" and can move to independent work. Anyone who finishes the work early moves on to a prepared "next step" activity and works on it until Ms. Moore calls the whole class back together for full-group sharing about the independent task.

Like-Pattern Groups

Although self-assessment of general understanding works well in some scenarios (such as readiness to begin an activity), it is often necessary for the teacher to conduct more concrete formative assessment to clarify the degree to which students have mastered key skills. When teachers analyze these formative assessment results and discover that different students need different feedback in order to move forward, they can place students in *like-pattern groups*. These groups are also known as "like-readiness groups"; they differ from a team huddle in that the entire class works in small groups on tasks that have been tailored to their most recent assessment-revealed needs.

Consider the example in Figure 3.11. This teacher begins the class by holding up the exit cards from the previous day and explaining that students were "all over the place" with this assessment. Therefore, they will be analyzing their assessment results with a partner (or two) to concentrate on taking their personal "next steps." The teacher then places students in like-readiness pairs or trios, returning their assessments to them, and instructing them to follow their task-specific directions (see Figure 3.11), which are either written or posted in a shared digital space. Students receive only *their* assigned task directions—not all three sets.

The teacher circulates, providing targeted assistance where needed, and closes the class by asking students to share "a-has!" from their work. If time permits, the whole class can set up and solve one of the problems generated from students completing Task 1. This is an efficient and low-pressure way to differentiate instruction.

Figure 3.11		
Like-Pattern Group Tasks		
Pre-Assessment Students are given three word problems and asked to set up and solve each.		
Pattern 1 Got It! (set-up and solved all three correctly)	**Pattern 2** Made Few Errors (in either setup or in solving)	**Pattern 3** Made Several Errors (in setup and solving)
Task for Pattern 1 You solved all three problems correctly. Now, with your group partners, make up three new word problems for others to solve: one that is harder than those you just solved, one that is at the same level, and one that is easier.	**Task for Pattern 2** ___ of the problems that you attempted are incorrect. With your group partners, identify the incorrect solutions and fix them (Wiliam, 2011).	**Task for Pattern 3** The highlighted portions of each problem show where you made errors. With your group partners, determine what those errors were and fix them.

Used correctly, like-pattern groupings will flex and flow throughout a unit of instruction. The examples in Figures 3.12 and 3.13 illustrate this principle in action at two different points within a middle school English language arts classroom.

The first set of tasks you see in Figure 3.12 was developed in response to patterns revealed by a short pre-assessment. Later in the unit, after students had more time to examine and practice using persuasive language, they revisited their pre-assessment responses and augmented them to reflect their growth. The teacher reviewed the augmented responses and used them to form *new* like-pattern groups for a second set of tasks (see Figure 3.13). Because students had multiple opportunities to practice and receive feedback between these two assessments, many of them changed readiness groups. In other words, composition of the like-pattern groups would be different in Task Set 1 and Task Set 2. Even if there is some overlap in a student's pattern-group assignment, changes in the grouping arrangement (quads vs. pairs/trios) and the equally respectful nature of the task options makes it unlikely that students will feel pigeonholed into a "low" or a "high" group.

Figure 3.12

Like-Pattern Grouping: Task Set 1

Pre-Assessment
Describe five ways that people use language to persuade others to believe their point of view. Then, use, underline, and label at least three of these techniques in a short paragraph in which you argue that "[*your favorite food*] should be served in the cafeteria every day."

Pattern 1	**Pattern 2**
Students describe and use at least two techniques accurately and effectively.	Students struggle to describe and use techniques effectively.

Task Introduction
Read: Mo Willems's *Don't Let the Pigeon Stay Up Late*
Discuss: The effectiveness of the pigeon's arguments
Take notes on: Persuasive techniques and logical fallacies

Task for Pattern 1 (Quads)	**Task for Pattern 2 (Quads)**
Using a series of Calvin and Hobbes cartoons (those featuring long, complex "rants"), determine the techniques Calvin uses, how effective they were and why, and what he may have done differently.	Work with another Pigeon book–*The Pigeon Wants a Puppy* (isolated speech bubbles)–to determine the techniques Pigeon uses, how effective they were and why, and the areas in which he's declined/improved.

Closure Activity
Mixed quads (representatives from Pattern 1 and Pattern 2 task groups) compare notes and see what Calvin and Pigeon have in common and what is distinct to each.

The progression of tasks from Figure 3.12 to Figure 3.13 underscores just how important it is to frequently gather and use formative assessment evidence to form like-pattern readiness groups. While a pre-assessment provides a good starting place for readiness grouping, it will not capture students' growth as the unit continues. Only recent formative assessment evidence allows us to create like-pattern groups and tasks that (1) capture the moment a student begins to "get it" and (2) foster that students' ongoing progress.

Learning Stations

The *learning stations* (or just *stations*) technique provides a flexible structure for managing simultaneous instruction, learning activities, or tasks. Stations can be used to introduce topics or concepts, provide opportunities for practice, or explore new ideas and skills (Doubet & Hockett, 2017).

Figure 3.13	
Like-Pattern Grouping: Task Set 2	
Midweek Formative Assessment Students receive their original pre-assessment (cafeteria paragraph) back and revise it to make their argument stronger. They include an annotation of why they chose the new techniques and discuss what would change if they were addressing the principal.	
Pattern 1 Revisions are sound and sophisticated. Voice and language change to suit audience.	**Pattern 2** Revisions lack sophistication. Voice and language remain the same.
Task for Pattern 1 (Pairs or Trios) Create two speeches arguing for a shorter school year: one for the school board and one for local businesses. Explain what you change from audience to audience.	**Task for Pattern 2 (Pairs or Trios)** Watch a video to review persuasive techniques. Create two speech outlines arguing for a shorter school year: one for the principal and one for parents. Explain the differences in your language.
Closure Activity A volunteer who completed the Pattern 1 Task shares their local-business speech; a volunteer who completed the Pattern 2 Task shares their parent speech. The class discusses how the language and techniques compare/contrast and why.	

The general method for structuring station rotations is to divide the class in thirds; during station time, one third works at a teacher-led station, one third works on independent tasks using technology, and the final third works in partners on collaborative tasks. To reduce the number of students at each station, the class can be divided in fourths instead—with the fourth station dedicated to small-group brainstorming or review tasks. In either case (thirds or fourths), the groups rotate so that every group visits every station within the class time (see Figure 3.14). This structure allows the teacher to differentiate instruction during the teacher-led rotation, which means that students would be working in like-readiness groupings (based on the skill the teacher will target at the teacher-led station) during all rotations. Since this is the case, the other stations can be customized as well, to make sure students work with materials and tasks that are tailored to support their growth.

Figure 3.14

Two Common Models of Learning Station Rotation

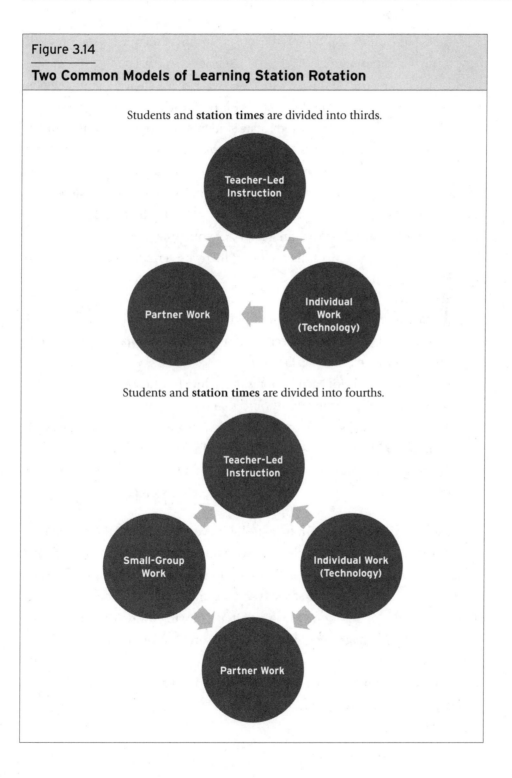

Students and **station times** are divided into thirds.

Students and **station times** are divided into fourths.

Although the thirds approach is the most common structure for station work, there are myriad variations (see Figure 3.15). If teaching with a partner (co-teacher, resource teacher, instructional assistant), two teacher-led stations would be possible for all students to rotate through. With two teachers, it's also possible to divide the class into four groups and rotate students between two stations in two different learning arrangements: each group switches between one teacher-led station and one independent or collaborative station. Alternatively, students can be grouped heterogeneously and rotated through three or four unsupervised stations; meanwhile, the teacher calls students (from all rotations) into a team huddle for more guided instruction, review, or enrichment.

No matter the structure of the rotations, there are certain station criteria that help maximize student focus and success:

- A procedure for communicating (and tracking—use a timer!) how much time students will spend at each station as well as signals to wrap things up and to rotate to the next station.
- Explicit directions for each station's procedure (written or recorded), along with all necessary materials, resources, and exemplars.
- A standard system students can use to ask questions and get help (e.g., write their name on the board, hold up a signaling stick, and so on).
- Accountability measures or something for students to produce at each station.

It's not necessary to reinvent the wheel for every station rotation. If students are engaged in ongoing tasks, such as working through a learning menu, or if they are deep into a lengthy project, one station can serve as dedicated work time for those pursuits. Station rotations reserved for guided and independent practice are also gaining popularity in schools that are moving away from homework. Consider how an arrangement like that might work with your own students and learning objectives.

To see the learning stations technique in action in both elementary and secondary classrooms, visit the links in Appendix D.

Figure 3.15

Two Alternative Models of Learning Station Rotation

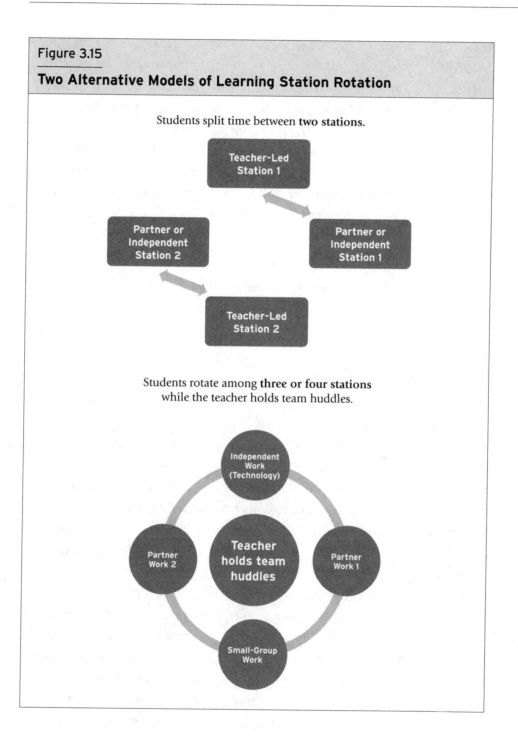

Students split time between **two stations.**

Teacher-Led
Station 1

Partner or
Independent
Station 2

Partner or
Independent
Station 1

Teacher-Led
Station 2

Students rotate among **three or four stations**
while the teacher holds team huddles.

Independent
Work
(Technology)

Partner
Work 2

Teacher
holds team
huddles

Partner
Work 1

Small-Group
Work

Stage 5's Formative Foundations strategies take the most time to prepare and the most flexibility to implement. However, once students are used to working with their classmates in configurations described in the other stages, Stage 5 groupings become less intimidating and more like just another thread in the fabric of the classroom. In addition, once the teacher becomes more comfortable using groups to address patterns, it's easier to spend more time on targeted feedback; this helps move every student forward, no matter their starting point.

The Progression at a Glance

Let's take a moment now to review the entire progression. Figure 3.16 provides a summary of the instructional strategies that can be used in each of the five stages of flexible grouping.

Standing Flexible Groups

Earlier in this chapter and before, in Chapter 2, I alluded to some grouping configurations that have not appeared in any of the stage discussions: Justin Minkel's reading groups, Ms. Dawkins's perspective groups, and Emily Knupp's PBL groups (pp. 26 and 50). Each of these groups stays together for a sustained amount of time (up to a month) with a specific goal in mind. We refer to such groups as *standing groups*. As long as standing groups are focused on a discrete criterion (e.g., mastery of a particular skill, exploration of a shared interest) and are used in concert with other kinds of groupings, they fit well into the schematic of a flexibly grouped classroom. However, if they are based on broad brush strokes of ability or are used as the sole means of grouping, they do not.

Consider Justin Minkel's reading groups. Over the course of a month, Justin used two types of standing groups for reading: fluency friends (five to six students with similar fluency skills) and book clubs (three to four students who chose the same book). In addition to those standing groups, he also implements fluidly grouped reading strategy circles, with a composition that changes frequently based on the latest evidence from observation and assessment. Finally, Justin groups students in math (according to readiness) and science (according to interest) so that everyone is consistently working with a variety of classmates.

Figure 3.16

The Progression of Flexible Grouping

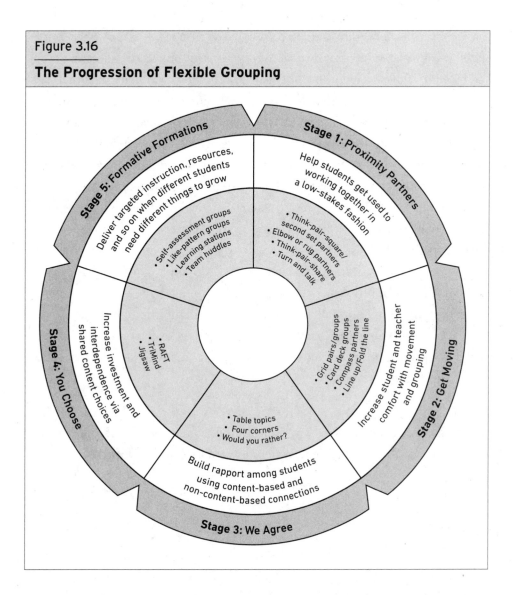

Like Justin's fluency friends groups, Ms. Dawkins's standing like-perspective groups were originally formed around the specific skill of *inferencing*; the students stayed together in the group not for a grading period but for a single unit. During this unit, students frequently reconfigured into several types of pooled perspective groups and into a variety of Stage 2 and 3 formations (e.g., fold the line, four corners, interest-based investigations). This kept Ms. Dawkins's groups fluid and ensured that students worked with a wide variety of classmates—not just those in their perspective groups.

Finally, consider Emily Knupp's project-based groups (see p. 50). She grouped students with shared interests into standing groups for project completion, but she used team huddles to regroup students in ways that would help meet their specific needs. In these "by invitation only" groups, she provided additional support or challenge as revealed by formative assessment or observation. She also held "open invitation" groups to share topics of interest such as research tools, helpful websites, and new apps that would enhance students' final products. When the students' projects concluded, the project groups disbanded, and Emily created *new* standing groups based on recent interest surveys. Students in her classroom knew they would get to work with each of their classmates at some point, so they stopped worrying so much about who was in which group at any one time.

Because the teachers and students in these three particular classrooms are familiar with and enthusiastic about flexible grouping, they can successfully use grouping formations from all five stages. It's important, though, for teachers to start in the stage where they feel best prepared and to keep working and remain in that stage until both they and their students are ready to step up to the next level of implementation.

● ◪ ⌛

In the next chapter, we will explore some of the management issues that prevent many teachers from taking the next steps toward a flexibly grouped classroom.

4

Procedures for Flexible Grouping

The teachers featured in this book use information about instructional purpose, student needs, and their own readiness to drive their decisions about why, when, and how to group. Less apparent, but equally important, is how they keep the cogs of a flexible grouping system well-greased and moving smoothly. For this system to operate as efficiently as possible, it's important to have procedures and routines in place for

- Setting the tone and expectations for flexible grouping.
- Laying the social foundation for flexible grouping and building upon it.
- Transitioning into and out of group arrangements.
- Structuring and launching flexible grouping tasks.
- Assigning and allowing choice of roles within groups.
- Monitoring progress, noise, and time.

This chapter will explore practical strategies and tools for each of these "nuts and bolts" procedural areas.

Setting the Tone and Expectations

On Day 1, let students know that they will be switching groups frequently. Your explanation of flexible grouping might sound something like this:

> In this class, you'll get the chance to work with many of your classmates in a variety of groups—from partnerships to groups of six or more. You might work with me, talk with one another, or collaborate on a task or project that requires each of you to contribute your skills and ideas.

Sometimes I'll choose the groups, and sometimes you will. And sometimes we'll let chance decide. My job is to switch these groups a lot so that you interact and learn from different people for different reasons, and so that they learn from you, too.

With this foundation in place, you can begin building students' collaborative capacity through informal groupings. Stage 1 and Stage 2 strategies are appropriate tools for this job: *think-pair-share* can facilitate brainstorming; *fold the line* partners can respond to posted questions or prompts. Another approach is to plan a "warm-up" schedule that could be conducted over one week of consecutive days or parsed out over two weeks:

- *Day 1/Grouping 1:* Students line up by birthdate (month and day) and form partners with the person to their right.
- *Day 2/Grouping 2:* Students receive a playing card and form same-suit trios.
- *Day 3/Grouping 3:* Students use their playing card from the previous group (or a new card) to form like-number quads.
- *Day 4/Grouping 4:* Students report to a corner of the room that corresponds with a favorite food; once there, they subdivide into pairs or trios.
- *Day 5/Grouping 5:* Students line up in "ROY G BIV" order by shirt color. The teacher then "folds the line" to form partnerships between students at opposite ends of the spectrum.

This approach "warms up" students not only to one another but also to the notion that they will be working with various peers in a range of configurations. In flexibly grouped classrooms, students are less worried about who is in which group, even when the teacher groups them by similar readiness level.

Laying the Social Foundation and Building upon It

Even a carefully considered combination of goals, task, and grouping doesn't ensure that students will want to interact with one another. Sometimes, peer interactions and collaboration falter simply because students don't know, like, or respect one another . . . *yet*. Teachers must "till the soil" to prepare students to work interdependently with classmates whom they may or may not consider friends. Whole-class sharing and community-building activities are critical tools in a flexibly grouped classroom because they provide ways for students to both establish their individuality and find areas of common interest with peers. A few tried and true activities that can help accomplish these goals include the following:

- *Student surveys*—Use prepared forms like the one in Figure 3.4 (see p. 40) to gather details about students as individuals and allow them to share their responses with one another.
- *Attendance questions*—During roll call at the beginning of class, students respond not with the standard "Here!" but with the answer to an announced question: favorite color, cereal, animal, movie, or game; Saturday or Sunday? Dogs or cats? Coke or Pepsi?
- *Pie charts*—Students divide a circle into five "slices" that proportionally illustrate their hobbies or how they spend their free time.
- *Me bags*—Each student is given a paper bag to fill with three to five items that best represent who they are. They can share and explain their items, or the teacher can share each bag and ask the entire class to guess who each bag belongs to.

It's also a good idea to begin the year establishing norms for group interactions. One middle school teacher began the year by placing students in groups to *silently* assemble simple jigsaw puzzles (without a map). They completed three rounds, trying to beat their own time with each progression:

- *Round 1*—Each group worked on a single puzzle (starting with the pieces face down) using only nonverbal communication.
- *Round 2*—The puzzles rotated so that each group received a new puzzle. The procedure was the same as Round 1, except that groups could discuss strategy before they flipped the pieces over and began assembly.
- *Round 3*—Once again, puzzles rotated, and students followed Round 2's procedure, but this time, they could talk *during* puzzle assembly.

The class debriefed after the experience and compiled a list of helpful strategies employed during the competition, such as "Everyone took on a different role," and "We communicated clearly, both verbally and nonverbally." The teacher recorded students' responses, tweaking them as necessary to keep them general, and used the list as guiding "group interaction norms" for the year (see Figure 4.1). Thereafter, students referred to their own recommendations to guide effective collaboration in all kinds of grouping configurations.

Figure 4.1
___
Group Interaction Norms

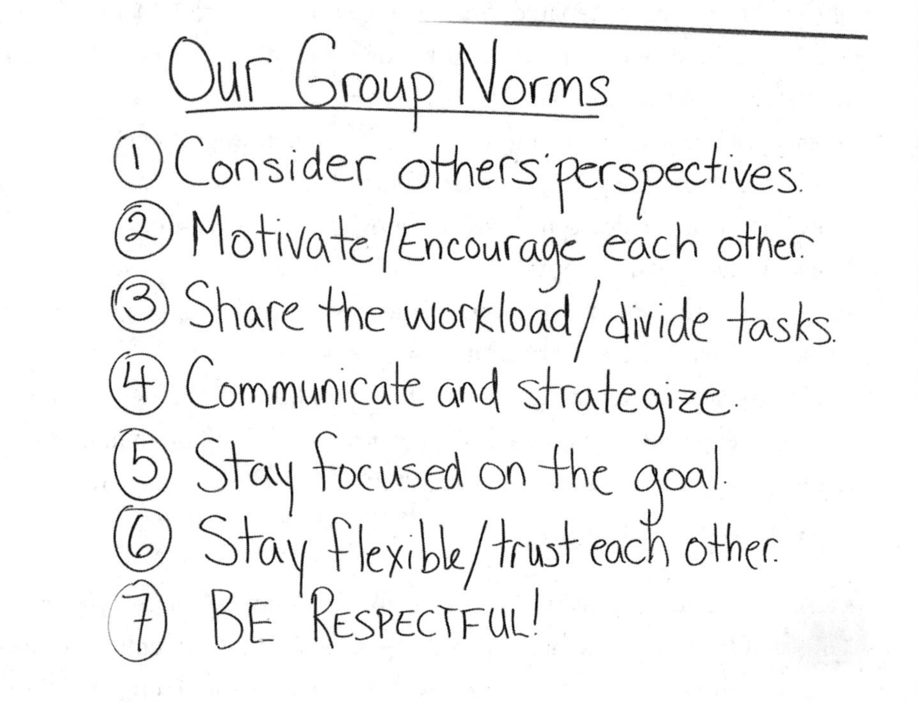

<u>Our Group Norms</u>
1. Consider others' perspectives.
2. Motivate/Encourage each other.
3. Share the workload/divide tasks.
4. Communicate and strategize.
5. Stay focused on the goal.
6. Stay flexible/trust each other.
7. BE RESPECTFUL!

Beyond the initial getting-to-know-you efforts, smaller, deliberately planned, group-level bonding moments help groups gel, release tension, and exercise courtesy. Examples of these might be opening prompts like, "Before you start your work on this paired task, share your favorite ice cream flavors," or asking students to bump elbows as they complete each step of the task. Teachers can also display fun anchor questions for students to discuss once they are finished—some related to the content or task (e.g., "Where have you seen this topic portrayed in real life or in the media?") and some simply appealing to general interests (e.g., "If you could have any superpower, what would it be and why?"). As the year continues, strategies from Stage 3 (e.g., table topics, four corners) can further students' efforts to connect with one another.

Modeling Successful In-Group Interaction

It's important for students to *see* and *experience* (not just *be told*) how to implement discussion strategy procedures effectively. Fleshing out what group norms (such as those in Figure 4.1) look like in action during instruction will support ongoing success throughout the rest of the year.

So, for example, ask volunteers to act out example and non-example conversations with "elbow partners" while the rest of the class takes notes on how well those conversations uphold group norms. Post or provide sentence frames for students to use as scaffolds during group dialogue. Consider posting the prompts like these to guide group conversations:

- What do you think about _____? Why?
- Where in the text does it show that?
- I agree with you about _____, but I disagree that _____.
- Can you explain your thinking about _____?
- You made a good point when you said _____ because_____.
- I saw that differently. Here's my take:_____.
- Can you give me an example of that?
- Thanks for a good discussion, [name].

Upfront investments like these are instructional time savers in the long run. It's much easier to *remind* students of routines during complex tasks (e.g., refer them to an anchor chart or a previous experience) than to try to *teach* both the routines and the tasks at the same time.

Providing Guidance for Successful Transitions

In a flexibly grouped classroom, students will change groups several times per week or even per day; providing visuals to guide student movement is a must.

It's a good idea to have areas of the room clearly delineated so that movement to those areas can be automatic. Ms. Forbes, a high school teacher, hangs different-colored paper lanterns above clusters of desks in her classroom. She easily regroups students by projecting a slide with students' names in their color groups; they know to move to the pod of desks under the blue lantern, the green lantern, and so on. Middle school teacher John Hostetter follows a similar approach, hanging colored and labeled paper signs above tables; this also helps his English language learners remember color names. Mr. Winston's students create "name plates" by decorating half sheets of paper with their names and any designs or symbols they like; when he changes group formations, he places those name plates on desks so that students know where to sit. Megan Jackson places numbered table tents on each table so that she can direct students to the proper location when they enter the room or when they change groups during class. In Figure 4.2, you can see photos of each of these strategies. Other ideas include projecting group names on the board or using flexible grouping charts (with moveable student pictures or names attached to clothespins or by magnets or Velcro).

It's also important to establish locations in the room for materials and devices, along with procedures for handing them out. Once there is a system in place, you can devote the first few days of class to conducting dry runs: students moving in an orderly way from place to place at set signals, students retrieving and returning materials and technology appropriately, and so on.

Structuring the "Launch" of Group Tasks

Guidance for how students will move into groups must be accompanied by clarity on what they are supposed to do when they get there. It's a good idea to begin with a brief, general overview of the goals and procedures; then, provide more detailed task instructions to each group. It's best to discuss *only full- or all-group procedures* during the general overview and to save group-specific instructions for distribution to those appropriate groups. This will keep students focused on their own group's task rather than on what everyone else is doing.

For group tasks, the more structure, the better. Anticipate and address potential questions and areas of confusion by providing checklists, visuals, or recorded instructions for groups to listen to on devices. Recorded Flipgrid or Seesaw videos of your instructions can serve as "mini-teachers" at each group space, freeing you to circulate and put out fires where needed. You might also institute a "1-2-3, then me" approach to questions about the task: students take one minute to read the directions silently, two minutes to discuss the directions with one another or with other groups, and three minutes to plan their approach to the task *before* they ask you for assistance.

If choices are involved (e.g., Stage 3's four corners strategy), consider asking students to secretly and silently "commit" to their choice on a sticky note (or use the "Hidden" setting on Padlet) before moving into groups. This helps ensure students are making their choice based on the *choice itself* and rather than who else in the class has or has not chosen it.

Figure 4.2

Transition Strategies

Assigning or Allowing Choice of Roles

When students assume unique roles in groups, they tend to take more ownership of their work. Roles can be *low stakes* (managerial tasks such as retrieving materials or prepping technology) or *high stakes* (academic or thinking skills such as analyzing or constructing). If the roles are low stakes, it makes sense to keep them engaging and fun. For example, if students are working in pairs, and each partner will do something different in the task, use "food group pairs" to designate those roles:

> OK, today's roles are Salt and Pepper. Decide who's Salt and who's Pepper. Salt, find the bookmarked article in Commonlit.org. Pepper, pull up the Google Doc named "Text Structures." You have one minute. Go!

Food group pairs (Peanut Butter and Jelly, Eggs and Bacon, Ketchup and Mustard, Macaroni and Cheese, Burger and Fries) could last the better part of the year! Or, for variety, you could throw in dynamic duos from pop culture (Batman and Robin, Sponge Bob and Patrick, Bert and Ernie), literature (Frog and Toad, Frodo and Sam, Holmes and Watson), and so on.

Cooperative learning traditionally has roles, but assigning one student to be the "leader" and another to be the "recorder" sends a clear message about which role (and which student) has higher status. Take care that all group roles are important and worthy of respect. Middle school teacher Kyle Asmus uses the following roles in his randomly formed cooperative groups (Edutopia, 2018):

- *Scribe*—Records group thinking on standing whiteboards.
- *Speaker*—Presents findings at the end of an activity.
- *Inquirer*—Asks the teacher questions when the group gets stuck or needs clarification.
- *Manager*—Keeps the group on task; retrieves and replaces materials.

These roles work because each is necessary to the overall success of the group. Appendix D includes a link to a video showcasing Mr. Asmus's role assignments in action.

For high-stakes tasks (lengthier or more complex), be purposeful and strategic in your role designations. Think about the nature of the task, and identify which roles are naturally embedded within it. For example, when examining a political cartoon, you may need an *Eagle Eye* (to note the subtleties of the piece), a *Historian* (to research the cartoon's context), an *Art Expert* (to examine other work by the same cartoonist), and an *Opposition Researcher* (to find cartoons that represent opposing viewpoints). Each of these roles is equally important and worthy of respect.

Once roles are set, you might allow students to choose which of them they would prefer to take on, or you could assign them; the choice depends on the nature of the task and on how well you think students understand their personal strengths. To help yourself better understand everyone's strengths, invite students share their areas of expertise (see Figure 4.3 for an illustration).

Figure 4.3

Classroom Expert Chart

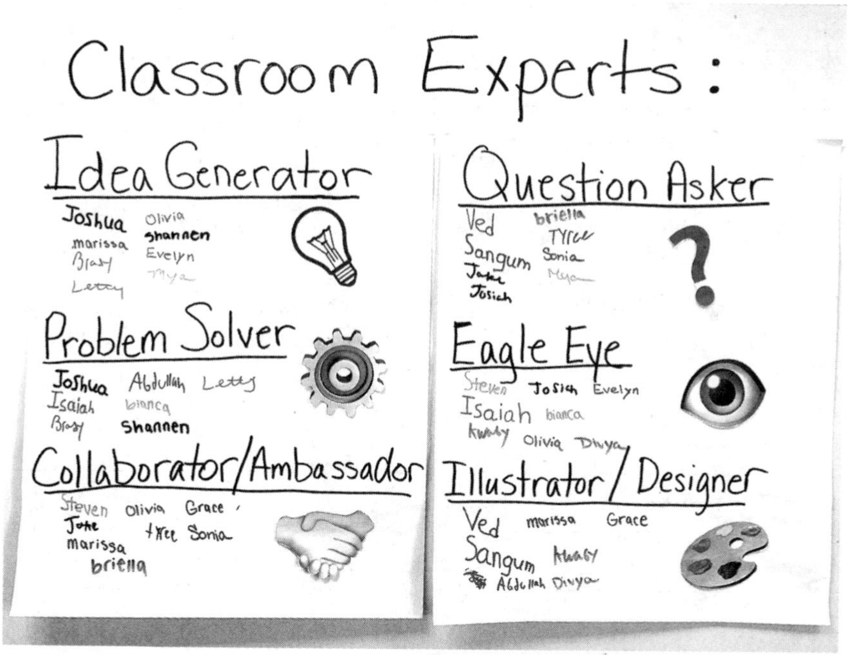

Another effective strategy for role creation and assignment is to establish several roles that students adopt on a regular basis—every time they read or listen to a text, every time they watch a video, and so on. Figure 4.4 spotlights four roles (with prompts) that students can take on when interacting with a source. All students should have the chance to "try on" all four roles; after that, they can choose their roles for given tasks, alternating between their favorites and those that

Figure 4.4

Roles and Role Prompts

Fortune-Teller

Look for clues or hints that might help us make predictions about . . .

_____

_____

_____

_____

_____.

Matchmaker

Find connections between_____

_____and_____.

How are they alike and different?

_____

_____

_____.

Detective

Capture the parts that best help us understand. . .

_____

_____

_____

_____

_____.

Defender

Agree or disagree?_____
Support your opinion with reasons.

_____

_____

_____

_____

_____.

Source: From *Differentiation in the Elementary Grades: Strategies to Engage and Equip All Learners* (p. 131), by K. J. Doubet and J. A. Hockett, 2017, ASCD. Copyright 2017 by ASCD.

push them outside their comfort zone. The most important aspect of assigning roles is ensuring all students contribute important pieces to the whole so that their groupmates need them to ensure a "360 degree" understanding of the topic.

Establishing and Ensuring Accountability

Accountability in group arrangements can be established in many ways; as discussed above, assigning roles is one approach, but the ideal technique will depend on the instructional purpose for the grouping and the nature of the task.

In Stage 1 groupings, the share phase can serve as the accountability step. For the other stages, a good rule of thumb is that if students have to work toward *producing* something—something to submit, present, or share with another group—they are less likely to spend time in off-task conversation. Products should require all group members' participation or contribution. Less formal products, like share-outs, might involve taping a piece of poster paper in the middle of the table and giving each student a different-colored marker to record ideas or giving each student a personal whiteboard and a dry-erase marker where they can write their responses. Alternatively, the product might be a graphic organizer that every student completes or a Google Docs slide to project or share with the teacher and classmates.

If students are doing their own version of the task (for example, completing their own graphic organizers rather than one organizer per group), announce that you'll be collecting one paper per group—but you won't reveal *whose* paper until the end of the activity. When time is up, use random criteria ("the tallest person in the group" or "the person with the birthday closest to today") to determine whose paper it will be. The randomness helps to keeps all students on their toes and encourages group members to support one another.

You can also use random criteria to select an "ambassador" from each group—a person who will rotate to another group, share their home group's findings, receive feedback, and either listen to or critique the work of the group they are visiting. When time is called, ambassadors return to their home groups and share insights gained in their "travels." All groups have the opportunity to use this new information to revise their thinking or work before submitting or presenting it. Alternatively, entire groups can rotate around the classroom to see work completed by their classmates and to leave both strength- and growth-based feedback. Appendix D includes a link to a video example of the latter "respond, reflect, and review" approach.

There are times when *discussion*, rather than production, is the goal of the activity. In those cases, ask students to rate the quality of their discussions using guidelines like those in Figure 4.5 or a rubric like the one in Figure 4.6.

If students are completing work on electronic devices, they should be able to submit their responses electronically. If students are working in pairs and groups on a particular skill, it makes sense for each of them to independently complete an exit ticket showing they can transfer their understanding to a new problem or context. To monitor student understanding, math teacher Denika Gum checks in with them when they leave their partner work station. Each individual student completes a new problem on a sticky note and places it on a group chart in an assigned and numbered spot. Denika uses her tablet to take a picture of the group's assembled exit tickets, and then, using her device's edit mode, makes notes about who she needs to check in with the next day and why.

Figure 4.5	
Discussion Guidelines—Elementary	
In a group discussion we . . .	
🗣	Share ideas that help us understand the topic.
☝✌	Give examples to help make our point.
👂	Listen to our classmates without interrupting.
🧑🧑	Use our classmates' names when adding to their ideas.
?	Ask our classmates questions in order to understand them better.
☺	Use facial expressions and body language to communicate respect.

Remember that *accountability* and *grading* are not synonymous. As the examples above demonstrate, you can build accountability steps into a lesson or activity without assigning a grade to it. See Chapter 5 for more discussion of grading in a flexibly grouped classroom.

Figure 4.6		
Discussion Rubric—Secondary		
Expert	**Accomplished**	**Growing**
• There was an energetic exchange of ideas among all members of the group. • Participants listened carefully with the intention of learning from one another. • Participants built on one another's ideas, deepening the conversation. • Participants asked clarifying questions, such as "What did you mean by...?" • All contributions were valued. • All exchanges (verbal and nonverbal) were respectful.	• All members of the group contributed ideas and examples. • Participants did not "talk over" others. • Participants took turns sharing ideas but did not really "discuss" or carry the thread of an idea forward. • Participants asked questions to engage others, such as "What do you think about...?" • Most contributions were valued. • Most exchanges (verbal and nonverbal) were respectful.	• Some members of the group did not contribute ideas, examples, or questions. • Participants interrupted others. • Conversations tended to veer off topic. • Participants rarely asked one another questions. • Participants rarely built upon the ideas of others. • Some contributions were valued. • Some exchanges (verbal and nonverbal) were disrespectful.

Dobbertin & Doubet, 2005.

Empowering Students to Monitor Progress, Time, and Noise

Enlist students as partners, if not primary agents, in keeping tabs on their group's progress, task time, and noise level. If groups are engaged in a multistep task, encourage them to keep a running list of what has been done and what is left to do. Individual group checklists or a master class list can serve this purpose; Trello.com offers a digital way to do both (you can find a link in Appendix D). To foster a sense of accountability, establish the norm that any group member can be called on to give a progress report at any time.

Giving students the responsibility to self-monitor does not mean leaving them completely to their own devices. Make sure students have a system to access help from you, whether by writing their names on the board to form a "teacher queue" (find a link to a demonstration in Appendix D) or by placing their "share sticks" (see Chapter 3, p. 32) in a "Help Me!" cup.

You can help students (and yourself) keep track of time by displaying an online digital stopwatch or another easy-to-see timer. Check in with students when time is running low to see if groups require more time by asking, "Fist to five—how many more minutes do you need?" If some groups finish before others, be ready with a next-step question or task for students to tackle.

Finally, a teacher in a flexibly grouped classroom will likely need to partner with students to develop strategies for dealing with noise. It's important to candidly discuss and establish guidelines for how much noise is appropriate and acceptable in different settings. Many teachers use descriptors to communicate suitable levels of noise for different kinds of work. Partner work may require students to use "inside voices" or "three-foot voices" (i.e., "I shouldn't be able to hear you if I'm more than three feet away from you"). Larger groups may use "dinner table voices" or "four-foot voices." It's also important to establish signals for regaining students' attention while they are completing a group task. Clapping responses, flickering light switches, and other such audio or visual cues can help a teacher quickly gather the whole group for further instructions or to issue a "noise check." A site like bouncyballs.org (there's a link in Appendix D) provides a visually appealing way to both gauge and respond to the volume of the room. As students grow more comfortable with each other and with grouping, guidelines for noise will likely need to be revisited and revised to accommodate teacher and student needs. Finding that "just right" level is an ongoing process, but a worthy pursuit.

The nuts and bolts of grouping are many and varied, but they all rely upon healthy student–teacher partnerships for their success. Including students in the logistics of forming, maintaining, running, and evaluating the health of many and varied grouping structures makes the classroom feel like a shared space physically, intellectually, and relationally. And a shared space is a place where everyone has ownership and where everyone feels at home.

● ◪ ⊠

As you have seen in Chapters 1–4, there is a process for planning and implementing flexible grouping that begins with purpose, flows through group formation and use, and attends to the nuts and bolts of effective execution. But even if teachers take all of those principles and practices into account, some "what ifs" may remain—"what ifs" that might discourage some from taking the leap into flexible grouping. The next chapter will attempt to address some of those lingering questions and concerns.

5

Troubleshooting
Flexible Grouping

Ultimately, teachers pursue change with the goal of making the classroom work for every learner. Implementing flexible grouping can do just that! But every change brings with it areas of uncertainty for teachers who are truly concerned about getting it "right." This chapter explores the answers to some of the questions educators often have about flexible grouping, including concerns about *equity* (student status in grouping, for example), meeting the *special learning and environmental needs* of certain students, and *logistics* such as grading and integrating flexible grouping into online learning environments.

Concerns About Equity and Fairness

Aren't mixed-readiness groups always better? Don't like-readiness groups spotlight who is in the "high" and "low" groups?

In short, no. As discussed in Chapter 3's coverage of Stage 5 (Formative Formations), within a flexibly grouped classroom, like-readiness groups are actually like-*pattern* groups, created to reflect students' most recent assessment results. The composition of these groups changes from skill to skill, topic area to topic area, and—depending on the frequency of formative assessment—even from day to day.

Used in combination with groupings from the other four stages, like-pattern groups don't relegate some students to the "low" group and some to the "high" group. Further, since flexible grouping means the teacher is seeing students in a variety of grouping combinations, students' strengths tend to surface more readily than in a classroom with static grouping, whether it's statically homogeneous or statically heterogeneous. A teacher in a flexibly grouped classroom soon learns to hold high expectations for *all* students. Perhaps this is why studies of the effects of within-class readiness groupings are so promising (see Lou et al., 1996), showing positive effects on academic achievement for students at all levels, including students identified as gifted (Steenbergen-Hu et al., 2016).

One of the primary arguments against exclusive use of heterogeneous groups is that it limits the academic growth of the gifted population (Fielder et al., 2002). It's said that academically advanced students end up teaching other students in their group and seldom, if ever, take their own next steps toward greater expertise. Additionally, the argument goes, students in heterogeneous groups who are consistently challenged to work "above" their readiness level can grow discouraged by always needing to be "taught" by the more advanced students. Many of these students eventually shut down and let their groupmates do the work (Robinson, 1997). In contrast, like-readiness groups give the teacher opportunities to provide *targeted feedback to all students,* one of the highest impact factors in Hattie's (2009, 2012) metanalyses of strategies that impact student growth.

The practice of flexible grouping should quiet these concerns. The bottom line is that when students work in a variety of grouping configurations—sometimes grappling with content beyond their comfort zone, sometimes being the expert, sometimes pursuing their specific interests—labels and restrictive roles and expectations fall away. Chapter 2's look into Ms. Dawkins's classroom (see p. 26) spotlights a unit implemented with 8th grade students. The students worked in like-readiness pairs and groups, but they *also* worked in several different mixed-readiness grouping configurations where they could share their unique perspectives. The status differences that had been highlighted in their exclusively heterogeneous cooperative teams became indistinguishable. And the students noticed: "In this unit, there weren't groups of smart or dumb people; just people who knew different things," one said at the conclusion of the unit. "Yeah," her classmate agreed. "You could always ask someone with more inside information [if you were stuck]" (Dobbertin & Doubet, 2005).

There is a place for both like- and mixed-readiness groupings in a flexibly grouped classroom. Used in combination and with other groupings, they diffuse status differences and highlight the authentic contributions of all learners.

Can flexible grouping help me create a more culturally responsive classroom?

In part, yes. Implementing flexible grouping is an important step in the journey toward a less biased, more inclusive, anti-racist classroom (Facing History and Ourselves, 2019).

First, flexible grouping is a way to maintain high expectations for all students and avoid pigeonholing students into static roles or groups. It is a tool for spotlighting, celebrating, and leveraging student strengths, and in that way, it can help to broaden many schools' narrow conception of what "smart" is. What's more, by bringing all kinds of students together, flexible grouping is a way to reveal shared interests among students who may believe they have nothing in common. Flexible grouping also capitalizes on the highly "collective" or communal orientation characteristic of most African, Asian, Latin American, and Middle Eastern cultures. These collective cultures emphasize "relationships, interdependence within a community, and cooperative learning" (Hammond, 2015, p. 25).

However, *flexible grouping alone is an insufficient tool to combat racism.* As teachers, we must also dedicate ourselves to actively dismantling our own biases, be they overt or hidden. We must have conversations about our anti-racist work with our students. (Appendix D provides a link for guidance in both areas.) In addition, we need to search for ways to illuminate how students' interests, backgrounds, and cultures connect to what we teach. Finally, we should consistently make sure our curriculum reflects contributions from and positive representations of diverse authors, thinkers, and producers in the field. As Beverly Daniel Tatum explains, students need to both *see themselves* in the "picture" of what they study and see themselves *looking good* in that picture (Rebora, 2019).

Concerns About Students with Special Learning Needs

What about students who are learning English? How do I meet their needs in a flexibly grouped classroom?

The general guidance for grouping English language learners (ELLs) is to place them in heterogeneous cooperative learning groups according to language needs (Hill & Flynn, 2014). Working in such configurations requires students to speak English, which in turn helps them develop their language skills. But making this the *only* way teachers group ELLs means considering only one aspect of these students' learning profile (language) and disregarding their readiness for content-related learning goals, their interests, their personal strengths, and so on.

In essence, it's treating "a communications issue as a cognitive one" (Checkley, 2015, p. 6) and equating students' readiness for English with their readiness for academic content and skills. This can produce "long-term negative effects on students' achievement and future educational opportunities" (Lee, 2012, p. 66), as it lowers the expectations others have for them and denies them access to rich learning experiences.

So how do teachers use grouping to meet students' academic needs while also addressing their linguistic development? In essence, it boils down to the guidance presented in Chapter 2. First consider the purpose of the task, and then consider which student characteristics factor most in achieving that purpose.

Here are some questions to ask yourself during planning:

- *Do students need to speak English in order to meet the task's learning goals?* If so, form linguistically diverse groups; if not, consider letting same-language peers sort through difficult content before sharing ideas in English. (*Note:* Although the practice was once discouraged, allowing students who are learning English to use their first language as scaffolding is gaining acceptance in the field [Williams, 2016].)

- *If you use exit slips or written assessments as the primary means of guiding your readiness grouping, will students' proficiency writing in English prevent them from "showing you what they know"?* If so, allow students to respond to questions and prompts out loud (by telling you or by recording themselves using Flipgrid or other recording apps and extensions). Use these responses to form readiness groups (like or mixed). This is a simple way to focus on academic skills and understanding without language skills interfering with assessment validity.

- *Do English language learners have the supports they need to interact successfully with the content and a diverse range of groupmates?* In any kind of grouping, provide English language learners with materials to scaffold their understanding, including leveled texts, highlighted texts, visual cues, sentence frames, frontloaded critical vocabulary and transition words, and so on (Williams, 2016). Keep in mind that these same scaffolds may help other students, as well (see the next question, which focuses on students with special needs).

- *What strengths do your English language learners bring to the specific tasks?* Consider their cultural expertise, their interpersonal skills, their content knowledge and enthusiasm, and their other habits of mind. In the crush of instructional planning, sometimes a focus on meeting a specific need that a population shares can keep us from seeing these students as complex individuals who have other tools that help them—and others—thrive.

- *Will the task require specific linguistic skills?* Call team huddles (see Chapter 3) with your English language learners when there's a specific linguistic need to address or when these students need a safe space to practice content-embedded language skills they will need in their group interactions.

The most important thing to remember, no matter what grouping configurations you choose, is that our English language learners are *more than simply English language learners;* they are three-dimensional human beings with areas of strength, struggle, interest, and passion. This was the message Claudette Monroy (2012), a thriving professional whose family moved from Mexico to the United States when she was in 6th grade, stressed in a guest lecture she gave at James Madison University. "The teachers who made a difference recognized that I wasn't just a kid who couldn't speak English," she said. "They saw that I was someone who could think. They had high expectations and asked me to do worthwhile things."

What about students receiving special education services? How do I respond to their IEP requirements and other learning needs in a flexibly grouped classroom?

In some cases, flexible grouping can facilitate teachers' responsiveness to the needs of students with disabilities. Of course, the first step is to regularly review students' individualized education programs (IEPs) to remain ever mindful of how best to champion their success. In this review process, make a note of accommodations that can be delivered via flexible grouping. Many of the recommendations from Chapters 3 and 4 (providing choices, collecting data, providing feedback, using a timer to stay on deadline, and so on) may actually appear as accommodations in students' (IEPs) (Morin, n.d.). Further, many studies have demonstrated that "peer-to-peer supports yield powerful academic and social benefits for students with disabilities" (Jung et al., 2019, p. 55). In short, strategic grouping supports students with disabilities.

For strategic grouping advice, refer once again to Chapter 2's planning procedure: First consider the *purpose* of the task then consider which student characteristics play the biggest role in making sure students achieve that purpose. In general, teachers should group according to *academic need* rather than diagnosed *special need.* In other words, we should still assess students' readiness for a task via formative assessment rather than base this decision on a label; not everyone with the same label is in the same readiness "spot" on any given day. Further, relying on labels rather than on needs "can too easily marginalize and hurt rather than help" (Jung et al., 2019, p. 18). Students who struggle to read, to pay attention, to sit still, to carry out complex instructions, and so on, still possess storehouses of strengths that teachers can tap into. Nevertheless, there are special circumstances to consider, some of which overlap with the considerations for students learning English. Here are some questions to ask:

- *Is reading or writing proficiency serving as a barrier to your attempts to gauge readiness through formative assessment?* If so, allow students to respond to questions and prompts out loud (by telling you or by recording themselves using Flipgrid or other recording apps and extensions). Use these responses to guide their readiness group placements.
- *Do students have the supports they need to interact successfully with the content and a diverse range of groupmates?* In any kind of grouping, provide necessary scaffolded materials including leveled texts, highlighted texts, visual cues, technology-based writing assistance, and so on. Focus on supports that directly assist the student in fulfilling the task requirements. Keep in mind that these same scaffolds may also help students who do not receive special education services; the more accessible content is to the broadest range of students, the better for all.

It's easier for a teacher to provide IEP and Section 504 accommodations in the context of grouping if they have established the expectation at the beginning the year that everyone in the class is on a journey toward expertise; some just might take different routes to get there. Andrew Lough illustrates this idea in his classroom by actually challenging his students to use a GPS system to find at least three different routes to a location he provides: the quickest route, the route that avoids interstates, the route with the most scenic stops along the way, and so on. Before long, students have explored a variety of paths to the same destination. Andrew then explains that the same principle holds true for his class; everyone is pursuing the same goals, but they will take different routes to get there. "So, don't be surprised if you have different tasks or materials than your classmates," he says. "It's all about the GPS!"

Grouping, of course, can present special challenges for some students with emotional and behavioral disorders and for some students on the autism spectrum. Although teaching social skills is woven into the fabric of a flexibly grouped classroom (see Chapter 4), some students need more scaffolding with these skills than others (Loftin et al., 2005). In such cases, keep these guidelines in mind:

- If you have a student who is particularly fascinated with a topic, whenever possible, find ways to link to that fascination in your interest-based choices (Kluth, 2010). Even though a student on the autism spectrum who perseverates on colors and the color wheel may be the only one who chooses to research the topic option "Color symbolism in Orwell's *1984*" when *like-interest* groups meet, they will be able to share their findings in *mixed-interest* groupings.
- Favor the use of pairs instead of groups for students who get overwhelmed by too many people and too much sensory input.
- Identify several students in the class who are willing to serve as "buddies" for students with special needs during group work; then rotate those buddies so that all students work with a variety of peers.
- Establish quiet spaces in your classroom where students can move when overwhelmed. Such quiet spaces, "calming corners," or "Zen zones" can help students refocus before returning to a group *or* serve as an alternate workspace, if needed.

In general, it's important to remember to remain flexible. *All* students, including students with special needs, have both good days and bad days. If it's a good day, help them stretch themselves by working with a partner or in a trio. If it's a bad day, let them work in a way that's comfortable (i.e., independently) for a while before stretching toward interaction. Everyone has a next step to take, but the size and shape of those steps need not be the same.

Concerns About Logistics

Should I grade group work? If so, how?

If you examine the five stages of group work in Chapter 3, you'll find that almost all of them involve sense-making, or *processing*. In other words, those tasks represent the *journey* toward mastering the learning goals rather than the *destination*, mastery itself. Because the majority of students' grades should reflect the degree to which they have arrived at the destination, these more formative, journey-based tasks need not be graded.

That's the short answer, but there are exceptions. To address them, let's back up a little. In general, grading should reflect three aspects of student learning, known as "the three P's" (Guskey, 1996; Tomlinson & Moon, 2013):

- *Performance*, or how well the student met the teacher-identified learning goals (mastery of key knowledge and skills)
- *Progress*, or how much growth students experienced through the process of completing a task or project.
- *Process*, or the habits of mind that help students achieve success (e.g., active engagement in group work, responding to feedback, asking for assistance when needed).

Using this framework, most group tasks could provide *progress* or *process* data, both of which are more qualitative in nature and not easily represented by a letter grade. This is why, in addition to accountability purposes, it's important to ask students to produce something during their group work or for the teacher to sit in on discussions and use rubrics like those featured in Figures 4.5 and 4.6 (see pp. 72–73) to make notes about student contributions. Data gathered through work samples and observation help inform our assessment of students' progress and process.

Stage 4's "You Choose" strategies, however, may be handled differently. While the jigsaw, RAFT, and TriMind examples featured in Chapter 3 were used to help students make sense of content or to practice skills, these same frameworks *could* be used to develop summative assessments (complete with rubrics) that students complete independently (Doubet & Hockett 2015, 2017). In this situation, the individual grade becomes a performance grade; groups are used simply as a mechanism for sharing and closure.

Project-based learning (PBL) presents additional considerations. Student work on a PBL should include both individual and group components as part of students' grades. Evaluation tools like those in Figures 5.1 and 5.2 can be useful for evaluating both the individual and group aspects of the performance so that data can be reported and considered separately (in light of which of the three P's each represents).

Figure 5.1			
Self-Evaluation Tool for Collaboration			
Component	**Expert Collaboration Criteria**	**Notes on My Areas of Strength**	**Notes on Room for Growth**
Doing my job	*During this group project, I . . .* ☐ Completed my assigned task thoroughly, accurately, and on time. ☐ Paid close attention to success criteria for my assigned task. ☐ Helped my teammates complete their tasks if I finished early. ☐ Helped evaluate the final product according to success criteria, demonstrating a willingness to revise, if necessary.		
Sharing the mic	*During this group project, I . . .* ☐ Actively listened as much as I spoke. ☐ Genuinely considered and reflected on ideas from all team members. ☐ Remained flexible to accommodate different styles of thinking, working, and processing. ☐ Pursued group consensus with perseverance and patience.		
Respecting my peers	*During this group project, I . . .* ☐ Spoke respectfully to my teammates. ☐ Refrained from interrupting. ☐ Provided honest feedback in a constructive way. ☐ Set aside minor disagreements ☐ Leaned into discussions of important differences of opinion with grace and dignity.		

Figure 5.2			
Group or Peer Evaluation Tool			
Component	**Expert Collaboration Criteria**	**Notes on Our Areas of Strength**	**Notes on Our Room for Growth**
Doing our jobs	*Teammates . . .* ☐ Completed their assigned tasks/ portions thoroughly, accurately, and on time. ☐ Demonstrated close attention to success criteria for their assigned task/portion. ☐ Helped their teammates complete their tasks/portions if they finished early. ☐ Evaluated the final product according to success criteria, demonstrating a willingness to revise, if necessary.		
Sharing the mic	*Teammates . . .* ☐ Actively listened as much as they spoke. ☐ Genuinely considered and reflected on ideas from all team members. ☐ Remained flexible to accommodate different styles of thinking, working, and processing. ☐ Pursued group consensus with perseverance and patience.		
Respecting one another	*Teammates . . .* ☐ Spoke respectfully to one another. ☐ Refrained from interrupting. ☐ Provided honest feedback in a constructive way. ☐ Set aside minor disagreements. ☐ Leaned into discussions of important differences of opinion with grace and dignity.		

How do I find time for all this grouping? I only have a 45-minute class period!

It's important to think of flexible grouping as occurring *over time*. It makes more sense to plan for flexible grouping over the course of one to two weeks, a month, or a unit than it does for a day. Rather than race to create grouping configurations on a daily basis, proactively consider your lesson plans in "chunks," and plan your approach to ensure it is balanced, manageable, and will work to your students' best advantage.

First grade teacher Justin Minkel (see p. 26) planned his groups to flex and flow over the course or a month or two, and they flexed and flowed *across* subject areas rather than just *within* them, with like-readiness pairs in math, interest-based research trios in science, and both readiness-based fluency friends groups and interest-based book clubs in language arts. In the secondary grades, many teachers find success by planning for groupings to flow and change over the course of an entire unit of instruction. In a 45-minute class model, it might mean groups changing two or three times per week. If you teach on a block schedule, you might find that changing groups halfway through the lengthy class period "resets" attention and increases student productivity.

The important thing to remember is that flexible grouping should help you address your learning goals, not detract from them. Change group configurations with the frequency best suited for your context—your grade level, subject matter, students, and class length.

How do I stage multiple groupings if I don't have tables in my classroom?

Classroom space can present a logistical challenge, especially for those teachers whose classrooms feature rows of desk-chair combinations with little space on the room's perimeter. One middle school teacher in circumstances like this taught her students to report to their regular assigned seats, complete their warm-up, then move their desks into the posted configuration before traveling to sit in their assigned groups for the day. For partner work, students knew which two desks to place side-by-side. When asked to "square up," students knew which desks to move into quads. When directed to form concentric circles for fishbowl discussions, students knew which desks to move to the inner circle and which desks to move to the outer circle. Of course, this took some rehearsal, but the teacher found that, as with most management procedures, work invested on the front end paid off in efficiency and the reduction of conflict later on. You can find a link to additional seating arrangements ideal for small classrooms in Appendix D.

Is it possible to flexibly group in an online/blended environment?

Yes, it is possible! Not every strategy discussed in this book will translate to an online environment, but some absolutely will. Let's quickly go through all five stages of group work and identify the techniques within each that translate to remote settings. Keep in mind that (1) we will change our notion of "groupings" to "interactions" (to account for the lack of physical proximity) and (2) these interactions can take place in both synchronous (e.g., Zoom meeting rooms) and asynchronous (e.g., posting and commenting) environments.

Stage 1: "Proximity Partners." Although students won't necessarily be next to one another, they can engage in quick *turn and talks* (see p. 31), if the teacher puts them in randomly paired breakout rooms in Zoom, Microsoft Teams, and so on. It's still a good idea to give students a warm-up prompt ("McDonald's or Burger King?") to answer before discussing the content-focused prompt(s). Students can also meet in more formalized partnerships (*elbow/rug partners;* see p. 31), if the teacher sets those up ahead of time. Warm-up prompts aren't necessary for established partners, although they are usually fun and seldom a bad idea.

Stage 2: "Get Moving." Two strategies in this stage—*grid pairs* and *compass partners*—can be used to structure student interactions in asynchronous settings for commenting and providing peer feedback. As a reminder, to determine grid partners (see Figure 3.2, p. 36), the teacher creates and shares a chart with each student's name listed in one square on the grid with blanks below each name. Older students can use this grid to make sure they are commenting on a variety of peer's posts (e.g., in discussion posts or on Padlet or Flipgrid). Students comment on a classmate's post and record the date on the first blank below their name to document their partnership. The next time students are asked to comment, each finds a new classmate to respond to and again records the date. Unless absolutely necessary, students should comment on a new classmate's post each time grid pairs are called until they have commented on posts from everyone in the class; after that, they can use the second blank below each classmate's name to start over a second time, and so on. For students in the younger grades, the teacher can assign grid pairs for comments or other interactions, making notes about who worked with whom to ensure a variety of partners. Alternatively, students can use a simplified *peer interaction Bingo card* (see Figure 5.3) to "mix themselves" up as much as possible.

Compass partners (p. 35) work well for peer review, a process that requires a little more trust building. Students and teacher can use a guide like the one in Figure 3.3 (see p. 37) to form these ongoing partnerships, and the teacher can ask students to share their drafts (via Google Docs, etc.) with either a teacher-selected (East/West) partner or a student-selected (North/South) partner.

Figure 5.3

Peer Interaction Bingo Card

Try to get bingo by working with as many classmates as possible.

Adriana	Asia	Andrew	DaNae	D'Shawn
Heath	Jalen	Joshua	Mandie	Matthew A.
Matt H.	Mikayla	Natalia	Nick	Noah
Pedro	Rachael	Rhyan	Riya	Sarah
Seth	Sophie	Tori	Tyler	Zoya

Stage 3: "We Agree." The *table topics* strategy (pp. 38–39) is a great way to establish like-interest discussion groups or breakout rooms in synchronous class meetings. Using information from digitally collected pie charts or student surveys (see Figure 3.4, p. 40), the teacher can form like-interest groups for informal

processing chats or homework review. Those topics of interest can (but don't have to) be woven into the tasks themselves, such as examining the topography of the group's favorite vacation destination or examining the nutrition labels of their favorite foods.

Stage 4: "You Choose." Both Google Docs and Flipgrid are hospitable environments for *jigsaws*. The most efficient way to complete an online jigsaw is for each home group to create a shared Google Doc. "Experts" do independent research and enter their findings in the designated area of the shared document. Any question for group members can be posed in the Google Doc itself or through an email or group chat.

A variation that encourages more interaction involves students completing their "expert" tasks and then explaining their work in a Flipgrid post. Home group members watch their classmates' posts and take notes, commenting with insights or questions or sending those comments and questions to one another via email or a group chat. (You can find additional tips for digital jigsaws linked in Appendix). *DRAFT* and *TriMind* products can also be shared jigsaw fashion using either of these approaches.

Finally, students may simply want to choose their preferred digital workspace (access to teacher, access to peers, or silence). A link to a template for establishing each of these environments is included in Appendix D.

Stage 5: "Formative Formations." Like-pattern tasks can still be designed using data from online formative assessments. Tailored tasks can be assigned through Google Classroom, posted on different Padlets, or distributed using other focused means of delivery. *Team huddles* (pp. 49–50) also work well in online settings. The teacher should use standard language to introduce the purpose of a team huddle but also explain that the setting for each huddle may vary. For example, the teacher might reserve an online class/day exclusively for team huddles, and meet with each small group for a smaller chunk of time throughout the class or day. Alternatively, team huddles can be spread throughout a week of instruction, using breakout rooms or teams. Follow the link to a virtual "Breakout Room Choices" template in Appendix D for a structuring idea.

Online *learning stations* offer yet another forum for strategic grouping. A link to a virtual station template is also included in Appendix D.

What about student self-evaluation? It still has a place in an online classroom. Assessment groups like those that Shawna Moore uses (see p. 50) can be retooled as "traffic signals" (see Figure 5.4). The teacher would assign a task and invite those students who feel ready to begin (those who self-rated as a "1") to take the first "exit" and move to a breakout room to begin work. (The Breakout Room Choices template, linked in Appendix D, would work well in this scenario.) Students who have specific questions or who need material re-explained (self-rated "2"s) stay with the teacher in the main room, where they take turns asking their questions. When their questions are answered sufficiently, they take the second exit to begin work in a breakout room. The teacher is left with students who need a fresh take on the lesson (self-rated "3"s), so the teacher explains the material in a different way. If the lightbulb goes on at any point in the explanation, students take the third exit and move to breakout rooms to begin work. Those students who need additional help after the lesson reboot can stay with the teacher to begin work, although the teacher should first take a moment to visit the breakout rooms to check on students who exited earlier.

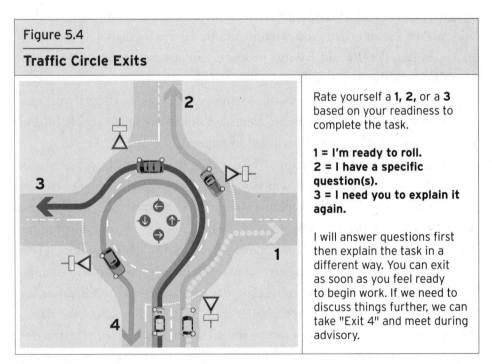

Figure 5.4

Traffic Circle Exits

Rate yourself a **1**, **2**, or a **3** based on your readiness to complete the task.

1 = I'm ready to roll.
2 = I have a specific question(s).
3 = I need you to explain it again.

I will answer questions first then explain the task in a different way. You can exit as soon as you feel ready to begin work. If we need to discuss things further, we can take "Exit 4" and meet during advisory.

Perhaps the most challenging grouping environment is the blended model, in which some students learn at home and some students (simultaneously) learn at school. In this case, one of the primary functions flexible grouping can serve is to build community among students in both settings. Following up whole-group instruction with partner practice that alternates between same-setting students and mixed-setting students (using individual devices) is one way to help all students feel part of the greater classroom community. Admittedly, it is tricky for teachers to circulate among both the physical and online spaces in order to make sure student interactions are productive. The good news is that teachers who have adopted and fine-tuned this "flexible partner" approach have found additional ways to group between settings, such as pulling small groups of both online and in-person students and using jigsaw strategically (with expert groups formed from like-setting students and home groups convening students from both settings). As is true in most teaching situations, success breeds success.

Structuring collaborative online interactions is not easy, but it's important to do anything and everything we can to make remote learning experiences engaging, meaningful, and targeted if we want students to show up, to thrive, and to grow. Just as with in-person groupings, teachers should start at the stage that's most comfortable and add to their repertoire as the year progresses. Trying to do everything at once will frustrate both the teacher *and* the students!

● ◪ ⧗

We have now examined how to plan for, implement, and troubleshoot flexible grouping. In the final chapter, we will revisit some familiar classrooms to see what this guidance looks like in action.

6

Portraits of Flexible Grouping

In the Introduction, we met several teachers who had adopted various approaches to instructional grouping as their classroom "norm." As the scenarios revealed, although these teachers used groups and realized benefits from their grouping practice ("glows"), they did not use *flexible* grouping, which left a number of positive opportunities ("grows") on the table.

Having explored the processes involved in making grouping more intentional, more fluid, and more flexible—and having seen examples of classrooms where grouping is flexible—let's revisit those earlier scenarios with fresh eyes and consider how these teachers could progress toward flexible grouping. We will (1) locate the grouping approaches of these teachers on the *progression of grouping* presented in Chapter 3; (2) review some suggested "next steps" in their journey toward expertise in flexible grouping; and (3) focus on how these adjustments have the potential to increase equitable learning opportunities for all students, referencing the **benefits of flexible grouping** introduced in Chapter 1.

Standing Reading Groups

Ms. Bonelli (see p. 2) relied exclusively on overall reading level to group students in her 1st grade classroom. Those groups remained largely static, with minor changes occurring in response to formal diagnostic testing (usually quarterly).

She recognized the efficiency of grouping students according to like-need for instruction, which seems to indicate she was operating in Stage 5 of the grouping progression ("Formative Formations"). However, because she relied on infrequent and nonspecific data to form these groups, she missed opportunities to provide more targeted instruction for *smaller skill components*, like fluency, decoding, and vocabulary. Further, the length of time students stayed together (from nine weeks to an entire school year) rendered her groups anything but flexible and limited students' chances to make connections and find commonalities with classmates outside their reading group.

Although, like Ms. Bonelli, Justin Minkel (see Chapter 2, p. 26) uses traditional reading groups with his young students, he also creates additional, more fluid reading groups that help him more frequently assess and address those smaller skill components. This enables him to gather students at different overall reading levels who all need to work on a similar discrete skill (such as fluency) and to work with them on that skill in a concentrated manner. In this way, he targets his instruction more efficiently than he could if he were working on fluency with generally leveled groups, in which students demonstrate a wide range of needs regarding the specific skill of fluency (Sparks, 2018). Justin's focus on targeting key skills lands his practice firmly in Stage 5 ("Formative Formations") group work for ELA as well as in math. In addition, Justin incorporates Stage 4 ("You Choose") groupings in ELA (book clubs) and in science (animal research); consequently, students consistently work with a variety of classmates over the course of a month, or even a week.

This is not to say that Ms. Bonelli should or even could implement all of these changes in her class; that would be overwhelming! But she could choose one area to "remodel" and start there, be it rethinking reading groups, adding formative formations for math instruction, or infusing interest-based groupings into ELA, math, science, or social studies. The payoff for such changes is a more equitable classroom that provides all students with opportunities for engagement, connection, and growth. Justin Minkel, whose classroom features a wealth of cultural and linguistic diversity, explains:

> There's an undeniable joy for kids of various levels in reading a "just right" book and talking about it with their classmates. That said, I think that the more flexible kinds of groupings . . . are important for a number of reasons. Kids who have an overall "high" level still often have gaps—say, with summarizing narratives or certain medial vowel combinations—that can persist if they don't have that kind of targeted "skill-specific" instruction. I also think it's important for "higher" and "lower" readers to work with each other for reasons related to class community, social-emotional development, and immersion for the struggling readers. In my class,

these struggling readers tend to be at lower levels of English acquisition, and they benefit from engaging in various kinds of conversations that feature richer and more varied vocabulary than they often get if they're always in a group with other struggling readers. (Personal communication, April 4, 2021)

Justin's discussion illustrates how a flexibly grouped classroom **grants access to equitable learning opportunities.** It helps students see one another as three-dimensional people rather than "the kids in the Blue Group." And that's vital for **combating status differences** that can arise and be reinforced in a classroom built solely around static grouping.

Socratic Seminar Circles

Even though Mr. Ross (see p. 3) teaches students who are much older than Ms. Bonelli's 1st graders, like her, he relies on a single approach to grouping. For him, it's the Socratic seminar. While Mr. Ross does conduct individual writing conferences one or two times each semester, his 12th grade English students spend the bulk of class time speaking in the circle or working independently on their essays. While working, students can ask questions of those seated next to them, which tells us that Mr. Ross is comfortable with the Stage 1 strategy of turn and talk. This is the only time the more reserved students speak, however, since the larger circle is an intimidating stage.

So what might be some appropriate next steps for Mr. Ross? First, he might consider reconfiguring his single circle into a fishbowl—two concentric circles. In this more complex Stage 2 ("Get Moving") strategy, each student in the center circle is partnered with a student in the outer circle (or with two students, depending on class size). Figure 6.1 provides a visual for this setup. The inner circle begins the discussion, while their partners in the outer circle take notes on big ideas from the discussion as well as their partners' performance—points of strength and ideas to consider. The discussion pauses for pairs to consult, and then resumes so that students in the inner circle can act upon their partners' feedback. The outer circle continues to take notes; they know they will soon be moving to the inner circle and want to be ready with ideas to contribute. The teacher pauses the discussion to "switch" circles, and the process repeats itself. (*Note:* If students are working in trios, the process repeats again.) Both the smaller circles and the "think time" in the outer circle encourage more reticent speakers to contribute.

Assigning partners for each discussion ensures students work with a variety of peers. In Appendix D, you'll find links to videos depicting the fishbowl strategy in action and a complementary "discussion mapping" strategy to help manage it.

Figure 6.1

Two Variations of the Fishbowl Strategy

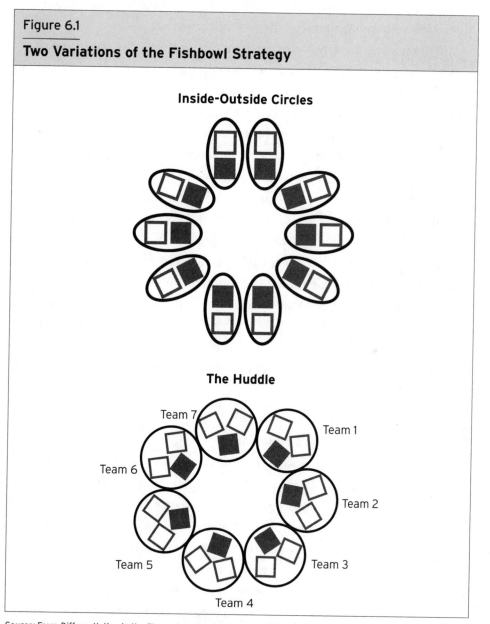

Inside-Outside Circles

The Huddle

A second step Mr. Ross could consider is to conduct his writing conferences in small groups rather than individually. Although he reads students' drafts before he meets with them to provide targeted feedback, he often finds he shares the same feedback with several different students. By grouping students with like needs together for a conference—a Stage 5: ("Formative Formation") pattern—Mr. Ross could use class time more efficiently *and* encourage idea-sharing and collaboration in revision both during and after the writing conference.

Implementing these two changes would alter the equity landscape of Mr. Ross's class by **increasing classroom camaraderie** in several ways. First, implementing the fishbowl version of the Socratic seminar changes the environment from one of competition to one of collaboration. The number of students vying for "airtime" is reduced to resemble more of a genuine conversation that might take place around a conference table or a dinner table. Further, during "consulting time," partner or trio-group members can provide speakers with encouragement ("You made a great point when you said . . ."), feedback ("You've used quotes to support your point two out of the three times you've spoken! Keep it up!"), and support ("Don't forget to bring up the point about . . ."). Second, writing conferences based on shared needs (e.g., organization, rich description) provide students with targeted feedback in the context of community. It's comforting for students to know they are in "good company" with the mistakes they've made, and it's helpful to have peer support while working through their teacher's feedback. In the process of sharing their writing, students also learn more about one another, **exposing them to divergent perspectives** and, in the process, **fostering empathy.**

Project-Based Learning Groups

Mr. Driver's use of project-based learning ensured that his 4th grade students would work collaboratively most of the time (see p. 4). Since students were united in their groups around a shared area of interest, his classroom exemplified Stage 4 of group work ("You Choose"). But his sole reliance on this grouping method meant he missed opportunities for more targeted skill work and magnified status differences by trying to meet a wide range of needs in a mixed small-group setting.

Recall Emily Knupp's approach to PBL in middle school (see Chapter 3, p. 50). While her standing project groups are also interest-based, she "mixes up" students regularly for skill-based small-group work based on formative and self-assessment evidence. This allows her to more efficiently (and more respectfully) address students' varying needs for support and challenge. Emily also allows each PBL group to send volunteers to serve as "ambassadors" for specific technology-based workshops (a Stage 3 "We Agree" formation; see p. 71). So, even though her project groups change with the same regularity as Mr. Driver's, her additional grouping structures ensure students work with a wider range of classmates along the way.

The flexibility Mr. Driver established using a project-based approach paves the way for him to seamlessly incorporate additional, more temporary Stage 3 interest-based groups and Stage 5's "Formative Formations." Expanding PBL to incorporate these additional grouping methods would make the classroom more equitable, as students have more opportunities to **encounter divergent perspectives.** Further, working with a variety of classmates within groupings formed for a specific purpose (to target a learning need, to address an area of interest) would increase opportunities to **cultivate growth** for all students in the classroom, even as they **strengthen classroom camaraderie.**

For additional resources on making the most of PBL, see Appendix D.

Cooperative Learning Groups

Ms. Williams used cooperative learning to group her middle school pre-algebra students (p. 4). In this model, students work in standing heterogeneous groups, usually for nine weeks at a time (Kagan, 2008). While cooperative learning has many social benefits, the snapshot in the Introduction illustrates its potential drawbacks, including creating and magnifying status differences and denying students with advanced understanding the opportunities to work with like-ready peers and receive the challenge they need to grow.

Fortunately, Ms. Williams need not throw out her cooperative groups altogether; she might simply supplement them with additional grouping formations. Cooperative groups function well as students' home groups, the configuration into which they move as they enter the classroom, begin their warm-up, and so on. But rather than remain in these same groups for every task (say, over an entire week or even during a learning block), students could disperse from their home groups into other configurations. To begin, Ms. Williams could follow her warm-up with some "Get Moving" activities from Stage 2 group work (e.g., fold the line, card deck groups) to explore new content. Later, she could provide processing options such as those discussed in Stage 4's "You Choose" tasks (e.g., TriMind, RAFT), with students moving from home groups into like-interest groups. Finally, when movement in and out of home groups becomes expected, Ms. Williams could begin to pull small groups into temporary homogeneous Formative Formations, where she would be better poised to provide tailored instruction to both support *and* challenge students with varying readiness levels.

It's important to remember that when targeted small-group instruction is provided to *all students*, it loses the "status sting" it carries when reserved only for students who struggle. In addition, it provides more appropriate next steps for all students, including those who need to be pushed further in their learning trajectories rather than exclusively serving as tutors for their classmates. Said differently, using cooperative learning to address varying student needs more strategically both **cultivates growth** *and* **combats status differences** in a purposeful way. Students lose the labels that can emerge from consistently "being taught" or from consistently "being the teacher." As one 10th grade student explained when describing his experience in flexibly grouped classes, "It doesn't make you feel like you're in smart classes or easy classes. When everyone [works] together, it's not really discriminating against you" (Doubet, 2007, p. 239).

Whole-Group Instruction

Unlike the other teachers we've met, 10th grade history teacher Mr. Pfeiffer seldom used any kind of grouping other than whole group (p. 5). His reliance on lecture and large-group discussion left little time and space for any kind of activity other than the occasional jigsaw to break up long readings. While large-group discussion has a time, place, and purpose, it cannot and does not suit all times, places, or purposes. Mr. Pfeiffer's assumption that his vocal students spoke for everyone was flawed; some students had opinions or questions they needed time to formulate before sharing; others struggled to maintain attention and missed large swaths of content; still others had misconceptions of which Mr. Pfeiffer remained unaware until he graded tests.

By incorporating a few "Proximity Partners" strategies from Stage 1 (e.g., think-pair-share and/or square), Mr. Pfeiffer could rectify each of these issues without much change to his customary planning and class setup. In addition, since he was already familiar with jigsaws, Mr. Pfeiffer's next step might be to use them as occasional alternatives to lecture, with the goal of allowing students to explore aspects of content that interest them. Using jigsaw as a Stage 4 "You Choose" strategy (like the example in Figure 3.5, see p. 43) rather than as a way to assign reading would motivate and unite students around shared interests rather than divide them over perceived skill differences. These two small changes would help Mr. Pfeiffer take large steps toward a more equitable learning environment for his students; both strategies give students multiple opportunities to process with their peers, which in turn **strengthens classroom camaraderie** and **exposes students to varying perspectives** beyond those of the teacher and the "vocal few."

Lab Partners

Lab tables aside, the classroom of AP Biology teacher Ms. Young (p. 6) looks a lot like Mr. Pfeiffer's. Driven by the AP exam looming at the end of the year, she avoids group work other than when she allows students to complete labs with partners. This may be due in part to the unfortunate reality that "textbooks present science as a solitary activity and not as what it actually is: a social process" (Kampourakis, 2013, p. 294). While the AP exam is, indeed, an individual pursuit, the nature of scientific inquiry is not (Bennet & Gadlin, 2012). This is most likely the reason both Ms. Young and her students prefer labs over whole-group instruction: as active, collaborative inquiry, it more closely mirrors the field of science.

For the non-lab portions of class, Ms. Young could start at Stage 1 and gradually work her way through the progression of all five stages described in Chapter 3. The kinds of group work featured in Stages 1 and 2 provide multiple ways to help Ms. Young and her students become more comfortable discussing science in smaller groups, where each voice can be heard. Strategies from Stages 3 and 4 provide opportunities for students to pursue inquiry in the company of peers who have similar questions. Once students are accustomed to more self-directed learning, self-assessment groups—a Stage 5 Formative Formation—would be a natural next step.

By providing multiple opportunities for her students to actively process information and receive feedback from their peers and teacher, Ms. Young increases the likelihood that students will do well on their exam (e.g., Bransford et al., 2000) and fall more in love with science in the process. Along the way, she'll be preparing her students for work in the real world. As one 11th grader explains, flexible grouping "helps me to learn how to work with other people who have different kinds of skills, opinions—just learn really how to work with a multitude of people" (Doubet, 2007, p. 239). This student's reflection illustrates that flexible grouping **strengthens students' capacity for collaboration,** which will serve them well for years to come.

What Are *Your* Next Steps?

Like the teachers featured in the Introduction and in this chapter, we all have areas of strength and areas for improvement when it comes to flexible grouping. The first step to growth is always honest evaluation of those areas. This starts with *self-evaluation,* (see Figure 6.2). The list of "look-fors" in Figure 6.2 can serve as a

Figure 6.2

Flexible Grouping "Look-fors"

The teacher . . .

☐ Establishes routines for moving into and out of groups, retrieving and returning materials, signaling for help or quiet, conflict resolution, and so on.

☐ Posts clear directions using multiple modalities (visual, written, recorded).

☐ Establishes a space for teacher-led groups that affords a view of the entire classroom.

☐ Frequently employs formative assessment (of readiness, interests, and learning preferences) to inform grouping choices.

☐ Demonstrates understanding of individual students' personalities, cultural norms, needs, strengths, likes, dislikes, and so on.

☐ Holds high expectations and provides important, engaging tasks for *all* students.

The students . . .

☐ Are "present" (physically, mentally, and emotionally) in group interactions.

☐ Use classmates' names often in conversation.

☐ Treat one another with respect.

☐ Seem to know, understand, and even enjoy one another.

☐ Move efficiently into and out of groups.

☐ Retrieve and replace materials efficiently.

☐ Use systems to signal and wait for help.

☐ Avoid interrupting teacher-led groups.

☐ Respond to noise cues and calls for attention.

☐ Resolve issues (instructional, logistical, and relational) with minimal teacher assistance.

The classroom features . . .

☐ Posted norms for group work and respectful conversations.

☐ Flexible seating (moveable desks or chairs).

☐ Flexible use of space (for large groups, small groups, stations, quiet work, etc.).

☐ Mechanisms for communicating fluid grouping configurations (hanging colored signs/lanterns, grouping chart, student pictures on magnets, names on clothespins, etc.).

☐ Supplies and materials accessible for self-service.

☐ Mechanisms for sharing work (whiteboards/desks, poster paper, virtual interfaces, Google Docs, etc.).

sort of evaluation instrument for that purpose. It can also facilitate a *peer evaluation* process, in which a colleague observes and provides feedback on their impression of strengths and next steps. Perhaps the most accurate (and admittedly, the most intimidating) evaluation can come from *students* themselves.

Recall from Chapter 1 the assertion that a good test of whether students have been grouped flexibly is to periodically ask them to make a list of their classmates' first and last names—or provide them with a version of the grid featured in Figure 3.2 (see p. 36 —and ask them to supply facts about each classmate (e.g., strengths, interests, favorites, hobbies). The results are a fairly dependable barometer for how flexible groupings really are. If students are unable to complete this task easily, you might want to consider shaking things up a bit more!

● ▨ ▧

As we move now to the end of the book and of our consideration of flexible grouping, the final question we'll explore is perhaps the most important: *Is it all worth it?*

Conclusion: Embracing the Promise of Flexible Grouping

As discussed in Chapter 1, flexible grouping has seven clear benefits:

- *It builds classroom camaraderie.*
- *It strengthens capacity for collaboration.*
- *It exposes students to varied/divergent perspectives.*
- *It fosters empathy.*
- *It combats status differences.*
- *It grants access to equitable learning opportunities.*
- *It cultivates growth.*

The examples and discussions throughout this book were intended to illustrate how these benefits might manifest themselves in the classroom. Generally speaking, you could this divide this list into *affective* and *academic* benefits, with the first five falling under the affective heading and the last two under the academic one. While both spheres are equally important, the affective benefits serve as a foundation for the academic benefits. Said differently, *when flexible grouping is used, the affective rewards set the stage for academic gains.*

Perhaps this is why Megan Wood, the principal of Lakeside Middle School in Albemarle County, Virginia, chose to frame her year-long professional development plan around flexible grouping. Her ultimate goal was academic gains for all students, but—because she was also "de-leveling" her classes—she knew those academic gains could only rise from a strong affective foundation (personal communication, August 6, 2020):

> We [administration and teachers] felt like we were tracking students . . .
> and so we agreed that eliminating levels would eliminate that aggressive

tracking. I was fearful that what teachers would do, though, is go straight to readiness grouping. While we had eliminated the [inequitable] structure in the schedule, I was terrified that they would replicate that structure in the classroom.

Ultimately, Megan wanted her teachers at Lakeside Middle School to *differentiate* their instruction to meet the wide range of student needs represented in their newly detracked classes, but she didn't want the levels to "reappear" in classrooms as static ability groups, similar to those employed by Ms. Bonelli, whom we met in the Introduction and checked in with again in Chapter 6.

In Chapter 1, we also explored the intersection of flexible grouping and differentiation, concluding that flexible grouping is a *principle* or *hallmark of differentiation* (Tomlinson, 2014), but it can also function as a *delivery system for differentiation*. The latter made sense to Megan from a professional development standpoint:

That's why I wanted to start with flexible grouping [rather than the other principles of differentiation]. If you start with the others, you risk living in the land of theory a little bit. Yes, all of the components make up a differentiated classroom, and yes, flexible grouping is one of those components, but I feel like it's the action component. I wanted teachers acting so they could then be reflecting on what worked and what didn't work.

Megan believed that the way to better equip Lakeside's teachers to address academic diversity was to give them time to get to know their students as people and foster genuine connections among students. Accordingly, the first few professional development sessions Megan set up focused on the first three stages of flexible grouping—"Proximity Partners," "Get Moving," and "We Agree"—stages that build classroom community by establishing and strengthening bonds among students and teachers. These stages were presented to Lakeside teachers not by lecture but through modeling and debriefing. By asking teachers themselves to engage in Stage 1, 2, and 3 grouping activities, Megan helped them learn by doing. She counts this as one of the most important components of professional development focused on flexible grouping.

If I am asking my teachers to [group flexibly], I better be ready to do it with them. I was really mindful whenever I did a PD session that whatever strategy I was trying to introduce them to, I had to implement that strategy in the session.

Allowing teachers to linger in those first three stages for a healthy chunk of time was a crucial component of Megan's approach with teachers. She recognized the need for teachers to have a strong foundation in the logistics of running groups before they could move on to the finer points of academic grouping. Megan also believed it would set the tone for teachers to move from deficit-based teaching to a more strengths-based approach. Flexible grouping is a powerful tool in fostering equitable learning experiences because teachers get to see students operating in a variety of configurations and roles. This creates situations in which talents that don't reveal themselves in individual work or that might be stifled when working with the same peers, day after day, have new ways to bubble to the surface. Invaluable strengths such as leadership, adaptability, creativity, problem solving, and so on are central to flexible grouping and, therefore, more likely to emerge in a flexibly grouped classroom. Megan understands this:

> That is how flexible grouping addresses the equity issue. It allows teachers to build off of students' strengths in a variety of ways. It builds a stronger classroom community, because kids are not interacting with the same people all the time. In powerful and productive ways, flexible grouping disrupts teachers' and students' views of themselves and of each other.

Once teachers and students were comfortable moving in and out of different groups for different purposes, Megan knew she had established the groundwork necessary to introduce (and model) the more academically focused Stages 4 and 5 strategies: "You Choose" and "Formative Foundations." Teachers were now ready—not just to learn about those new techniques but also to weave them in their classroom practices. Megan saw it happening during her walkthroughs. It looked like this:

> More interaction between students and higher levels of engagement. Teachers are starting to recognize that while it takes a lot of upfront work to do the flexible grouping in terms of planning, they're actually doing less work in the classroom, because the kids are engaging with the work more. I think teachers are surprised at how much more time has been freed up to check in with kids, gauge where they really are, and work with

them on an individual basis. I think they enjoy seeing kids build more autonomy and ownership over the stuff they are doing.

Megan's classroom walkthroughs revealed that, overall, Lakeside's teachers had become adept at grouping flexibly and were, for the most part, reaping the benefits. This doesn't mean that every teacher realized the promise of flexible grouping; just like our "portrait" teachers, Lakeside teachers were in different places in their personal journeys toward expertise and willingness to take risks. For example, a handful of teachers did not see the importance of the first few stages and began their grouping efforts with Stage 5 readiness arrangements. As expected, that backfired. Megan explains:

> Kids knew immediately how they were grouped, because they hadn't been doing the [other kinds of grouping]. I think that helped [those teachers] recognize why it's so important to flexibly group.

The bottom line is that *we can flexibly group without differentiating* (this looks like working exclusively in Stages 1, 2, and 3), and *we can differentiate without grouping flexibly* (this looks like working exclusively in Stages 4 and 5). But the true power to build classroom camaraderie, strengthen collaborative capacity, expose students to a variety of perspectives, foster empathy, combat status differences, provide access to equitable learning experiences, and support student growth lies in embracing all five stages. In doing so, we are more likely to create classrooms in which *all* students are able to showcase their brilliance (Hilliard, 2003).

So, choose a stage that feels right to you right now, commit to growth, and jump in! The current of community and possibility that flexible grouping generates will naturally keep propelling you and your students forward on your journey.

Acknowledgments

It is fitting that a project exploring the promise of collaboration would spring to life in partnership with so many generous colleagues and friends. I would like to express my heartfelt gratitude to . . .

Principal Megan Wood and the teachers (and librarian!) of Lakeside Middle School. Your dedication to serving your students and your openness to innovation spurred me onward throughout all phases of bringing this book to life. Thank you for allowing me to learn with and from you.

Justin Minkel and Emily Knupp. Your devotion to your students and your commitment to excellence on their behalf served as inspiration to me as I wrote. If I was stuck, I needed only to picture you in your classrooms to know what came next. Thank you for your expertise.

Genny Ostertag and Katie Martin at ASCD. You have been so much more than "editors" in this project; you have been vision-casters, thought partners, and encouragers. Thank you for sharpening me with your keen insights.

Katie Dredger (my department chair) and Ashley Taylor Jaffee, Zareen Rahman, Melanie Shoffner, and Angela Webb (my "self-study" buddies) at JMU. When I tried to throw in the towel, you caught it and gave it back to me. Thank you for encouraging me to press on.

Ann Allred, graduate assistant extraordinaire. Appendix D would not exist without you. Thank you for your attention to detail, your cheerful attitude, and keeping me on track.

Mindy Moran. Thank you for your unwavering honesty and your zeal for improving the landscape of education. Your resolve is inspiring.

Ed Brantmeier and Gilpatrick Hornsby. The JMU CFI virtual writing retreat you led was instrumental in reenergizing this project. Thank you for making that experience meaningful and productive at a time in the pandemic when that didn't seem possible.

Carol Tomlinson. Your discernment and encouragement pulled me through dark times and compelled me to move forward. You are the kindest and wisest of mentors (and of human beings). Thank you for being my sounding board, compass, and cheerleader. The depth of my gratitude is immeasurable.

Eldon and Susan Doubet, my parents. You love me unconditionally, support me extravagantly, and encourage me daily. Thank you for being my rocks.

Finally, this book is both testament and tribute to the faithfulness of God in my life. Soli Deo Gloria.

APPENDIX

Appendix A: Flexible Grouping Planning Template

			Notes About Assessments		
			Notes About Students		
Grouping Factors to Consider					
Use or Purpose of Grouping	Duration	Student Characteristics	Composition	Configuration/Size	Formation
• Building community • Practicing/applying skills; pro-cessing ideas • Investigating new content • Examining a text, data set, etc. • Peer review/feedback • Working on a project	• Less than a class period • A class period or two • Less than a week • More than a week	• Readiness/skill level • Interest • Preferred way of thinking/learning • Personal gifts/background/experiences	• Homogeneous (like) • Heteroge-neous (mixed)	• Partners • Trios • Small groups of ____ (4–5) • Circles of ____ (6–8) • Split class	• Teacher choice • Student choice • Random

continued

111

Task	Purpose and Duration	Characteristics and Composition	Size and How Formed	Summary of Learning Experience	Link to Groups
Task 1	Purpose: Duration:	Characteristics: Composition:	Size: How Formed:		
Task 2	Purpose: Duration:	Characteristics: Composition:	Size: How Formed:		
Task 3	Purpose: Duration:	Characteristics: Composition:	Size: How Formed:		
Task 4	Purpose: Duration:	Characteristics: Composition:	Size: How Formed:		
Task 5	Purpose: Duration:	Characteristics: Composition:	Size: How Formed:		
Task 6	Purpose: Duration:	Characteristics: Composition:	Size: How Formed:		

Note: Find a link to download a digital copy of this form in Appendix D.

Appendix B: Sample Flexible Grouping Plan—Elementary

Notes About Assessments

- Use pre-assessment of readiness to establish initial math and ELA groups.
- Use frequent ongoing formative assessment of readiness to adjust groups and form new groups for new tasks in math and ELA.
- Use task-specific interest inventories to form book groups in ELA and animal groups in science.

Notes About Students

In this class, many students are English language learners. Interviews and technology help collect formative assessment evidence so that academic needs are not conflated by linguistic needs. Extra supports for ELLs are offered within other grouping configurations. "Team huddles" provide opportunities for English language learners to preview topic-specific vocabulary.

Grouping Factors to Consider

Use or Purpose of Grouping	Duration	Student Characteristics	Composition	Configuration/Size	Formation
• Building community • Practicing/applying skills; processing ideas • Investigating new content • Examining a text, data set, etc. • Peer review/feedback • Working on a project	• Less than a class period • A class period or two • Less than a week • More than a week	• Readiness/skill level • Interest • Preferred way of thinking/learning • Personal gifts/ background/experiences	• Homogeneous (like) • Heterogeneous (mixed)	• Partners • Trios • Small groups of ____ (4–5) • Circles of ____ (6–8) • Split class	• Teacher choice • Student choice • Random

continued

Task	Purpose and Duration	Characteristics and Composition	Size and How Formed	Summary of Learning Experience
Task 1 **Math**	**Purpose:** Applying new skills in making arrays **Duration:** Extended math block	**Characteristic:** Readiness based on pre-assessment **Composition:** Like-readiness	**Size:** Partners **How Formed:** Teacher choice	• Preview the task by asking student volunteers to "fishbowl" –model a version of the task (with teacher direction). • Like-readiness pairs build arrays using the number of tiles assigned (smaller or larger of tiles; number adjusted to provide appropriate support or challenge). • Reconvene for partners to share work and discuss what they learned.
Task 2 **Science**	**Purpose:** Working on a project **Duration:** Several weeks (2–3 research days during science each week)	**Characteristic:** Interest **Composition:** Like-interest (animals), mixed-readiness (reading)	**Size:** Quads for research **How Formed:** Interest Inventory; rank animals to show first, second, and third choice of "favorites."	• Work with peers who have chosen the same animal (e.g., alligator, elephant, cheetah) as one of their Top 3 favorites. • Conduct structured research with tailored texts (tiered books, bookmarked websites, audio recordings of informational texts), and shared resources (videos, guest speaker). • Each group meets with teacher each workday to report progress and ask questions.
Task 3 **Science & ELA**	**Purpose:** Practicing writing skills **Duration:** One week	**Characteristic:** Readiness **Composition:** Like-readiness (writing)	**Size:** Varied **How Formed:** Teacher forms based on recent formative assessment/writing sample)	• Individually, each student creates their own "All About _____ [Animal]" book. • Call small groups of students together (from all animal interest groups) with like-need for workshops on using evidence from research and writing sentences. • Provide appropriate support and challenge.

	Purpose and Duration	Characteristics and Composition	Size and How Formed	Summary of Learning Experience
Task 4 ELA	**Purpose:** Practicing reading skills (fluency, decoding, vocabulary) **Duration:** Ongoing; a few times a week; changes frequently	**Characteristic:** Readiness **Composition:** Mixed-readiness but like-skill	**Size:** 5–6 students **How Formed:** Teacher created groups based on ongoing formative assessment	Begin with targeted instruction designed to improve fluency. Similar groups will form to target instruction in decoding and vocabulary. Pull "strategy circles" of varied sizes and compositions to deliver more targeted instruction around smaller skills like making inferences or sequencing. All groups formed according to recent, classroom-based formative assessment.
Other Potential Tasks				
To Precede Task 1 (Math)	**Purpose:** Investigating new content; building community **Duration:** One math period	**Characteristic:** Interest **Composition:** Like-interest; mixed-readiness	**Size:** Partners or trios **How Formed:** Student choice	• Label three corners of the room with words and pictures representing "Food," "Art," and "Toys." Students report to the corner they prefer. • Divide large interest groups into smaller pairs/trios. • Using tablet devices, present pairs and trios with digital images of arrays in the real world (in their chosen context). Students will discuss and describe each array and reproduce their favorites on graph paper.
To Follow Task 3 (Science & ELA)	**Purpose:** Peer-review of writing **Duration:** Less than one class	**Characteristic:** Interest **Composition:** Like-interest (animals)	**Size:** Whole class; pairs **How Formed:** Random partner from interest groups used in Task 3	As a full class, students use established "Look-Fors" (success criteria) to evaluate one another's work. (*Note:* Two to three writing "success criteria" are introduced to students early in the year, with others added as the year progresses.) After peers provide feedback as a class, students move into pairs to revise each partner's writing according to the class's suggestions.

continued

Other Potential Tasks	Purpose and Duration	Characteristics and Composition	Size and How Formed	Summary of Learning Experience
Any Time (ELA)	**Purpose:** Examining a text **Duration:** Several weeks, meeting several times a week	**Characteristic:** Interest **Composition:** Like-interest/book choice	**Size:** 3–4 students **How Formed:** Student choice of book for "book clubs"	"Book clubs" are formed when students choose the book they want to read and form groups with classmates who chose the same book. Books are united around a common *author* (e.g., Mo Willems), *theme* (e.g., friendship), or *topic* (e.g., dinosaurs). For this month's book club, students are reading their chosen *Don't Let the Pigeon . . .* book (by Mo Willems) and discussing both argument and design.

Source: Based on the work of Justin Minkel. Adapted with permission.

Appendix C: Sample Flexible Grouping Plan—Secondary

Notes About Assessments

Pre-assessment to determine:
- Students' interest in topics from history that serve as important background knowledge necessary to fully understanding the novel's context.
- Students' readiness to make inferences based on implied exposition in a text.

Ongoing assessment to determine:
- Students' favorite shows (for dialogue practice).
- Readiness to analyze the interdependence of literary elements in the book.
- Readiness to analyze and employ figurative language.

Notes About Students

One student in the class who is on the autism spectrum has a fascination with dates in history and prefers individual work. He proposed a different interest project for Task 1 below. He wanted to examine what was happening in the nation as a whole in the time period leading up to and encompassing when the book was set. He will study that on his own, then join a mixed-interest group for Task 2 to share his findings and make connections with the other students' projects.

Grouping Factors to Consider

Use or Purpose of Grouping	Duration	Student Characteristics	Composition	Configuration/Size	Formation
• Building community • Practicing/applying skills; processing ideas • Investigating new content • Examining a text, data set, etc. • Peer review/feedback • Working on a project	• Less than a class period • A class period or two • Less than a week • More than a week	• Readiness/skill level • Interest • Preferred way of thinking/learning • Personal gifts/background experiences	• Homogeneous (like) • Heterogeneous (mixed)	• Partners • Trios • Small groups of ___ (4–5) • Circles of ___ (6–8) • Split class	• Teacher choice • Student choice • Random

continued

Task	Purpose and Duration	Characteristics and Composition	Size and How Formed	Summary of Learning Experience
Task 1	**Purpose:** Working on a project (part 1) **Duration:** One week	**Characteristic:** Interest/choice **Composition:** Like-interest	**Size:** Groups of 3–4 (subdivided from larger groups) **How Formed:** Student choice of topic; teacher choice of groups	Students choose from and study these three topics*: • Jim Crow laws in Alabama at the time the novel was set • Poems and stories by black authors about that time period • The intersection of Monroeville, Alabama (Harper Lee's hometown) and the events described in Bryan Stevenson's book (and film adaptation), *Just Mercy*. *See "Notes About Students," above, for a fourth choice.*
Task 2	**Purpose:** Working on a project (part 2) **Duration:** Half a block period	**Characteristic:** Interest/choice **Composition:** Mixed-interest	**Size:** Trios or quads **How Formed:** Teacher forms so that each group has at least one of each choice represented.	• Students take turns sharing findings. • After each group member shares, the group compiles/adds to a list of (1) most fascinating things learned and (2) areas of overlap among the different groups' findings. • Discuss group findings as a whole class.

Task	Purpose and Duration	Characteristics and Composition	Size and How Formed	Summary of Learning Experience
Task 3	**Purpose:** Practicing the skill of making inferences based on implied exposition in a text ("like lens") **Duration:** Ongoing (more than once a week throughout the unit)	**Characteristic:** Readiness for inferencing **Composition:** Like-readiness	**Size:** 3–5 students **How Formed:** Teacher assigns students one of three "lenses" with varying complexities, and forms smaller "subgroups" of 3–5. Students meet in assigned groups to discuss chapters through their reading lens.	• *The Outsider:* Students who were able to glean insights from abstract text read the novel through the lens of Boo Radley to extract Boo's perspective on people, places, and events without direct evidence. • *The Wise and The Insider:* Students who were able to make "right there" inferences examine the text through the per-spective of either Calpurnia or Atticus Finch to determine the underlying meaning behind what they were and were *not* saying and doing. • *The Child:* Students who need support in making inferences read the text from Scout's perspective to determine "Does Scout really understand what's going on here? Why or why not? What does she get that adults do not?"
Task 4	**Purpose:** Examin-ing a text ("pooled perspectives") **Duration:** Ongoing (once a week throughout the unit)	**Characteristic:** Readiness for inferencing **Composition:** Mixed-readiness	**Size:** Quads **How Formed:** Teacher creates quads including at least one student from each reading lens.	• Pooled perspective quads closely examine key scenes from the vantage points of different characters (the Child, the Insider, the Wise, and the Outsider). • Each pooled perspective group meeting ends with a group synthesis statement summing up the key scene, conflict, or event in a way that reflects the perspectives of all characters.

continued

Task	Purpose and Duration	Characteristics and Composition	Size and How Formed	Summary of Learning Experience
Task 5	**Purpose:** Processing ideas/examining a text ("pooled perspectives") **Duration:** Ongoing (three times total for half of the block)	**Characteristic:** Readiness for inferencing **Composition:** Mixed-readiness	**Size:** Discussion circles of 6-7 students each **How Formed:** Teacher creates circles including at least 2 students from each reading lens	Pooled perspective discussion circles discuss overarching motifs and themes that emerge from the story over time. Students are to come to the circle ready to cite textual evidence from their assigned perspective. Each pooled perspective circle closes with a group synthesis product (group choice of form) that connects to a concept or addresses an essential question in such a way that it represents all perspectives.
Task 6	**Purpose:** Peer review/feedback **Duration:** Ongoing: use part of the block	**Characteristic:** N/A **Composition:** N/A	**Size:** Pairs **How Formed:** Randomly (using *line up*)	Students meet to peer review writing assignments, digital projects, and so on. Pairs are random, but success criteria/rubrics are consistent, facilitating efficient peer review.
Task 7	**Purpose:** Building community and practicing skills/processing ideas **Duration:** Occasionally for less than a class period	**Characteristic:** Preferred way thinking/learning **Composition:** Like or mixed	**Size:** Pairs, trios, or quads **How Formed:** Student choice	These activities occur throughout the unit, usually at the beginning of the period when students may participate in brief activities such as • *Four corners:* Students report to the corner that represents their favorite show and discuss with others (who chose that same show) how the characters, plot, and setting connect to the story's characters, plots, settings, and so on. • *TriMind:* Students choose from three options for analyzing figurative language in the novel and work with others who chose the same task to complete it.

Task	Purpose and Duration	Characteristics and Composition	Size and How Formed	Summary of Learning Experience
Task 8	**Purpose:** Processing ideas **Duration:** One class period	**Characteristic:** N/A **Composition:** N/A	**Size:** Split class and like-number quads (for *structured academic controversy*[a]) **How Formed:** Random[b] (*card deck groups*)	• Distribute playing cards to students upon entry. • Students gather into two large groups—even and odd numbers—to prepare to argue for or against the statement "*Things have [or have not] changed in the South since the time in which* To Kill a Mockingbird *was set.*" They must cite the novel and current events from reliable news sources. • Once cases are prepared, students gather in "like-number quads" to debate. The even numbers (supporting the claim) begin, followed by the odd numbers (refuting the claim). • Students switch perspectives and repeat debate.

Source: Dobbertin & Doubet, 2005.

[a]See Appendix D for a link to how to run a structured academic controversy.

[b]The teacher distributes cards strategically while maintaining the appearance of randomness.

Appendix D: Online Resources

Resource	Planning (Chapter 2) Link	QR Code
Flexible Grouping Planning Template	https://docs.google.com/document/d/17zr2cMW DM9dbFoT64wSBLuU4zSQeVnyjW1D6GdqzaOg/ edit?usp=sharing	
Structured Academic Controversy How-To's	https://teachinghistoryorg/teaching-materials/ teaching-guides/21731	

Resource	Progression (Chapter 3) Link	QR Code
Second-Set Partners	https://learn.teachingchannel.com/video/ second-set-partners-sfusd	
"Would You Rather...?" Questions	https://conversationstartersworld.com/ would-you-rather-questions/	
Self-Assessment/ Guided Groups in Action	https://www.teachingchannel.org/video/ guided-groups-formative-assessment	
Station Rotations Example (Elementary)	https://www.edutopia.org/video/station-rotation- differentiating-instruction-reach-all-students	

Station Rotations Example (Secondary)	https://www.youtube.com/watch?v=oY5iXxqe_WU	
Resource	**Procedures (Chapter 4) Link**	**QR Code**
Cooperative Learning Roles	https://www.edutopia.org/video/60-second-strategy-cooperative-learning-roles	
Respond, Reflect, and Review	https://www.youtube.com/watch?v=J4UQvt1Rn9w&list=PL10g2YT_In2hGQkIsIJxXMLY7wv6kFIUF&index=4	
Teacher Queue	https://www.edutopia.org/video/60-second-strategy-teacher-queue	
Resource	**Troubleshooting (Chapter 5) Link**	**QR Code**
"Self-Check" for Bias	https://www.edutopia.org/article/simple-way-self-monitor-bias	
Anti-Bias Teaching Activities	https://www.tolerance.org/magazine/antibias-teaching-just-got-easier	

Resource	Troubleshooting (Chapter 5) Link	QR Code
Flexible Grouping Seating Arrangements	https://www.teachstarter.com/us/blog/inspiration-for-classroom-seating-arrangements-2-2/	
Break-Out Room Choices Template	https://docs.google.com/presentation/d/1cnJeIJ755sYvEDTMmN5uQenDUsJtslv3xpSAGJH89BQ/edit?usp=sharing	
Virtual Stations Template	https://docs.google.com/presentation/d/1aDqYwwHZs4U-ZoNJ-1rdhSVZ11o2D-EMtoueJ-NX6UQ/edit?usp=sharing	
Jigsaw Method Online Adaptation: Google Slides Template	https://alicekeeler.com/2016/03/09/google-slides-jigsaw-activity-template/	
Online Teaching Adaptation: Jigsaw Video	https://www.youtube.com/watch?v=mKXY8DjtMHM	
Comprehensive Guide to Digital Learning	https://shop.ascd.org/PersonifyEbusiness/Store/Product-Details/productId/264442667	

Resource	Portraits (Chapter 6) Link	QR Code
Fishbowl Discussion Strategy in Action	https://www.edutopia.org/video/60-second-strategy-fishbowl-discussion	
Discussion Mapping in Action	https://www.edutopia.org/video/60-second-strategy-discussion-mapping	
5 Keys to Rigorous Project-Based Learning	https://www.edutopia.org/video/5-keys-rigorous-project-based-learning	
Comprehensive Guide to Project-Based Learning	https://shop.ascd.org/PersonifyEbusiness/Store/Product-Details/productId/264220909	

References

Batruch, A., Autin, F., Bataillard, F., & Butera, F. (2019). School selection and the social class divide: How tracking contributes to the reproduction of inequalities. *Personality and Social Psychology Bulletin, 45*(3), 477–490. https://doi.org/10.1177/0146167218791804

Bennett, L. M., & Gadlin, H. (2012). Collaboration and team science. *Journal of Investigative Medicine,60*(5), 768–775. https://www.ncbi.nlm.nih.gov/pmc/articles/PMC3652225/

Bransford, J., Brown, A., & Cocking, R. (Eds.). (2000). *How people learn: Brain, mind, experience, and school* (Expanded ed.). National Academy Press.

Brighton, C. M., Moon, T. R., Jarvis, J. M., & Hockett, J. A. (2007). *Primary grades teachers' conceptions of giftedness and talent: A case-based investigation*[Technical Report]. National Research Center on the Gifted and Talented.

Burris, C. C., & Welner, K. G. (2005). Closing the achievement gap by detracking. *Phi Delta Kappan, 86*(8), 594–598.

Checkley, K. (2015). Setting ELLs up for success. *Education Update, 56*(10), 1–7.

Cohen, E. G. (1998, September). Making cooperative learning equitable. *Educational Leadership, 56*(1), 18–21.

Cross, R., Rebele, R., & Grant, A. (2016, January–February). Collaborative overload. *Harvard Business Review,* 74–79. https://hbr.org/2016/01/collaborative-overload

Dabrowski, J., & Marshall, T. R. (2018, November). Motivation and engagement in student assignments: The role of choice and relevancy. *The Education Trust.* https://edtrust.org/resource/motivation-and-engagement-in-student-assignments/

Darling-Hammond, L. (1997). School reform at the crossroads: Confronting the central issues of teaching. *Educational Policy, 11,* 151–166.

Darling-Hammond, L. (2000). New standards and old inequalities: School reform and the education of African American students. *Journal for Negro Education, 69,* 263–287.

Deming, D. J. (2017). The growing importance of social skills in the labor market. *Quarterly Journal of Economics, 132*(4),1593–1640. https://doi.org/10.1093/qje/qjx022

Dobbertin, C., & Doubet, K. J. (2005). *To Kill a Mockingbird* unit. Created for *HOTTLINX study on differentiated instruction in middle school.* University of Virginia's National Research Center on the Gifted and Talented.

Doubet, K. J. (2007). *Teacher fidelity and student response to a model of differentiation as implemented by one high school* [Unpublished doctoral dissertation]. University of Virginia.

Doubet, K. J., & Hockett, J. A. (2015). *Differentiation in middle and high school: Strategies to engage all learners.* ASCD.

Doubet, K. J., & Hockett, J. A. (2017). *Differentiation in the elementary grades: Strategies to engage and equip all learners.* ASCD.

Duhigg, C. (2016, February). What Google learned from its quest to build a perfect team. *New York Times Magazine.* https://www.nytimes.com/2016/02/28/magazine/what-google-learned-from-its-quest-to-build-the-perfect-team.html

Edutopia. (2018, November 2). *60 second strategy: Cooperative learning roles* [Video]. https://www.edutopia.org/video/60-second-strategy-cooperative-learning-roles

Emdin, C. (2016). *For white folks who teach in the hood . . . and the rest of y'all too: Reality pedagogy and urban education.* Beacon Press.

Facing History and Ourselves. (2019). Lesson 4: Creating a classroom contract. https://www.facinghistory.org/back-to-school/download/Lesson_Plan_4_Creating_a_Classroom_Contract.pdf

Ferlazzo, L. (2017, February 25). Author interview: How the brain learns. *Classroom Q&A with Larry Ferlazzo.* https://blogs.edweek.org/teachers/classroom_qa_with_larry_ferlazzo/2017/02/author_interview_how_the_brain_learns.html

Ferlazzo, L., & Sypnieski, K. (2012). *The ELL teacher's survival guide: Ready-to-use strategies, tools, and activities for teaching English language learners of all levels.* Jossey-Bass.

Fielder, E. D., Lange, R. E., & Winebrenner, S. (2002). In search of reality: Unraveling the myths about tracking, ability grouping, and the gifted. *Roeper Review, 24*(3), 108–111.

Fish, R. E. (2017). The racialized construction of exceptionality: Experimental evidence of race/ethnicity effects on teachers' interventions. *Social Science Research, 62,* 317–334. https://www.sciencedirect.com/science/article/abs/pii/S0049089X15301642

Fisher, D., & Frey, N. (2021). *Better learning through structured teaching: A framework for the gradual release of responsibility* (3rd ed.). ASCD.

Gallagher, J. J. (1997). Least restrictive environment for gifted students. *Peabody Journal of Education, 72,* 153–165.

Gay, G. (2017). *Culturally responsive teaching: Theory, research, and practice* (3rd ed.). Teachers College Press.

Google. (2016). *Re:Work guide: Understand team effectiveness.* https://rework.withgoogle.com/guides/understanding-team-effectiveness/steps/introduction/

Groeger, L. V., Waldman, A., & Eads, D. (2018, October 16). *Miseducation: Is there racial inequality at your school?* ProPublica. https://projects.propublica.org/miseducation/?fbclid=IwAR0dyPs41_-OUiqsrgTV6Rh-iwmWVaAPWl3aBXQY1KjuIjhkjTALIMYMl1U

Guskey, T. R. (1996). Reporting on student learning: Lessons from the past—Prescriptions for the future. In T. R. Guskey (Ed.), *Communicating student learning: 1996 yearbook of the Association for Supervision and Curriculum Development* (pp. 13–24). ASCD.

Hammond, Z. (2015). *Culturally responsive teaching and the brain: Promoting authentic engagement and rigor among culturally and linguistically diverse students.* Corwin.

Hattie, J. (2009). *Visible learning: A synthesis of over 800 meta-analyses relating to achievement.* Routledge.

Hattie, J. (2012). *Visible learning for teachers: Maximizing impact on learning.* Routledge.

Hill, J., & Flynn, K. (2014). *Classroom instruction that works with English language learners* (2nd ed.). ASCD.

Hilliard, A. G. III. (2003). No mystery: Closing the achievement gap between Africans and excellence. In T. Perry, C. Steele, & A. G. Hilliard III (2003), *Young, gifted, and black: Promoting high achievement among African American students* (pp. 131–165). Beacon Press.

Jean, M. (2016). *Can you "work your way up?" Ability grouping and the development of academic engagement.* [Unpublished doctoral dissertation]. University of Chicago.

Jung, L. A., Frey, N., Fisher, D., & Kroener, J. (2019). *Your students, my students, our students: Rethinking equitable and inclusive classrooms.* ASCD.

Kagan, S. (2008). *Kagan cooperative learning.* Kagan Publishing.

Kampourakis, K. (2013). Mendel and the path to genetics: Portraying science as a social process. *Science and Education, 22*(2), 293–324.

Kelly, S., & Carbonaro, W. (2012). Curriculum tracking and teacher expectations: evidence from discrepant course taking models. *Social Psychology of Education, 15,* 271–294. https://doi.org/10.1007/s11218-012-9182-6

King, M. L. (1956, August 11). *The birth of a new age: Address delivered at the 50th Anniversary of Alpha Phi Alpha in Buffalo.* https://kinginstitute.stanford.edu/encyclopedia/king-delivers-birth-new-age-alpha-phi-alpha-buffalo-receives-award-honor

Kluth, P. (2010). *"You're going to love this kid!": Teaching students with autism in the inclusive classroom* (2nd ed.). Brookes.

Larmer, J., Mergendoller, J. R., & Boss, S. (2015). *Setting the standard for project-based learning: A proven approach to rigorous classroom instruction.* ASCD.

Lee, S. (2012). New talk about ELL students. *Phi Delta Kappan, 93*(8), 66–69.

Loftin, R. L., Gibb, A. C., & Skiba, R. (2005). Using self-monitoring strategies to address behavior and academic issues. In V. Gaylord, M. Quinn, J. McComas, & C. Lehr (Eds.) *Impact: Feature Issue on Fostering Success in School and Beyond for Students with Emotional/Behavioral Disorders, 18*(2). University of Minnesota, Institute on Community Integration. https://publications.ici.umn.edu/impact/18-2/cover

Lou, Y., Abrami, P. C., Spence, J. C., Poulsen, C., Chapbers, B., & d'Apollinia, S. (1996). Within-class grouping: A meta-analysis. *Review of Educational Research, 66*(4), 423–458. https://journals.sagepub.com/doi/10.3102/00346543066004423

McTighe, J., Doubet, K. J., & Carbaugh, E. M. (2020). *Designing authentic performance tasks and projects: Tools for meaningful learning and assessment.* ASCD.

McTighe, J., & Willis, J. (2019). *Upgrade your teaching: Understanding by Design meets neuroscience.* ASCD.

Monroy, C. (2012, October 12). *Lessons from an English language learner* [Guest lecture]. EXED 520: Differentiation of Instruction, James Madison University, Harrisonburg, VA.

Morin, A. (n.d.). *Common accommodations and modifications in school.* https://www.understood.org/en/learning-thinking-differences/treatments-approaches/educational-strategies/common-classroom-accommodations-and-modifications?_ul=1*169yhqr*domain_userid*YW1wLXVPcFFKOHJNOGdpUFVnSVJlTG81a0E.

National Academies of Sciences, Engineering, and Medicine [NASEM]. (2018). *How people learn II: Learners, contexts, and cultures.* National Academies Press. https://doi.org/10.17226/24783

National Association of Colleges and Employers [NACE]. (2018). *Job outlook 2019.* Author.

Oakes, J. (1985). *Keeping track: How schools structure inequality.* Yale University Press.

Oakes, J. (1997). Can tracking research inform practice? Technical, normative, and political considerations. In D. J. Flinders & S. J. Thornton (Eds.) *The curriculum studies reader* (pp. 247–265). Routledge.

Organisation for Economic Co-operation and Development [OECD]. (2010). *PISA 2009 results: What makes a school successful? Resources, policies, and practices (Vol. 4).* OECD Publishing. https://www.oecd-ilibrary.org/education/pisa-2009-results-what-makes-a-school-successful_9789264091559-en

Organisation for Economic Co-operation and Development [OECD]. (2012). *Equity and quality in education: Supporting disadvantaged students and schools.* OECD Publishing. http://dx.doi.org/10.1787/9789264130852-en

Perry, T., Steele, C., & Hilliard, A., III. (2003). *Young, gifted, and black: Promoting high achievement among African American students.* Beacon Press.

Rebora, A. (2019, April). Widening the lens: A conversation with Beverly Daniel Tatum. *Educational Leadership, 76*(7), 30–33.

Robinson, A. (1997). Cooperative learning for talented students: Emergent issues and implications. In N. Colangelo & G. A. Davis (Eds.), *Handbook of gifted education* (2nd ed.) (pp. 243–252). Allyn & Bacon.

RSA. (2013, December 10). *Brené Brown on empathy* [Video]. YouTube. https://www.youtube.com/watch?v=1Evwgu369Jw

Schofield, J. W. (2010). International evidence on ability grouping with curriculum differentiation and the achievement gap in secondary schools. *Teachers College Record, 112*(5), 1492–1528.

Slavin, R. E. (1996). *Education for all.* Swets & Zeitlinger.

Sousa, D., & Tomlinson, C. A. (2018). *Differentiation and the brain: How neuroscience supports the learner-friendly classroom* (2nd ed.). Solution Tree.

Sparks, S. D. (2018, August). Are classroom reading groups the best way to teach reading? Maybe not. *Education Week, 38*(2). https://www.edweek.org/teaching-learning/are-classroom-reading-groups-the-best-way-to-teach-reading-maybe-not/2018/08

Steenbergen-Hu, S., Makel, M. C., & Olszewski-Kuilius, P. (2016). What one hundred years of research says about the effects of ability grouping and acceleration on K–12 students' academic achievement: Findings of two second-order meta-analyses. *Review of Educational Research, 86*(4), 849–899.

Sternberg, R. J., & Grigorenko, E. L. (2007). *Teaching for successful intelligence* (2nd ed.). Corwin.

Teaching Channel. (2017). *Second-set partners: A turn-and-talk strategy* [Video]. https://learn.teachingchannel.com/video/second-set-partners-sfusd

Teaching Channel. (2018). *Guided groups for formative assessment* [Video]. https://learn.teachingchannel.com/video/guided-groups-formative-assessment

Terada, Y. (2021, February). New research makes a powerful case for PBL. *Edutopia.* https://www.edutopia.org/article/new-research-makes-powerful-case-pbl

Tomlinson, C. A. (2005, April 26). *Final class meeting: Addressing student questions* [Graduate course class discussion]. EDLF 739: Advanced Seminar in Differentiation of Instruction. University of Virginia, Charlottesville, VA.

Tomlinson, C. A. (2014). *The differentiated classroom: Responding to the needs of all learners* (2nd ed.). ASCD.

Tomlinson, C. A., Brimijoin, K., & Narvez, L. (2008). *The differentiated school: Making revolutionary changes in teaching and learning.* ASCD.

Tomlinson, C. A., & Doubet, K. (2005, April). Reach them to teach them. *Educational Leadership, 62*(7), 8–15.

Tomlinson, C. A., & Imbeau, M. B. (2010). *Leading and managing a differentiated classroom.* ASCD.

Tomlinson, C. A., & Moon, T. R. (2013). *Assessment and student success in a differentiated classroom.* ASCD.

Wiliam, D. (2011). *Embedded formative assessment.* Solution Tree.

Williams, V. (2016, February). Seven ways to scaffold for English learners. *ASCD Express, 11*(12). https://www.ascd.org/el/articles/seven-ways-to-scaffold-instruction-for-english-learners

Vygotsky, L. S. (1978). *Mind and society: The development of higher mental processes.* Harvard University Press.

Zimmerman, A. (2016, October). When is a student gifted or disabled? A new study shows racial bias plays a role in deciding. *Chalkbeat New York.*

Index

The letter *f* following a page locator denotes a figure.

About the Author

Kristina J. Doubet is a professor in the College of Education at James Madison University in Harrisonburg, Virginia, where she has received the Distinguished Teacher Award, the Madison Scholar Award, and the Sarah Miller Luck Endowed Professorship for Excellence in Education. As an independent consultant and ASCD Faculty member, Kristina has partnered with hundreds of schools, districts, and organizations around initiatives related to differentiated instruction, curriculum design using the Understanding by Design framework, performance assessment and project-based learning, formative assessment and feedback, digital learning, and classroom management and grouping.

In addition to authoring numerous articles in journals including *Kappan* and *Educational Leadership*, she is the coauthor (with Jessica Hockett) of *Differentiation in Middle and High School: Strategies to Engage All Learners* and *Differentiation in the Elementary Grades: Strategies to Engage and Equip All Learners*. She also coauthored *The Differentiated Flipped Classroom: A Practical Guide to Digital Learning* (with Eric Carbaugh), *Designing Authentic Performance Tasks and Projects: Tools for Meaningful Learning and Assessment* (with Jay McTighe and Eric Carbaugh), the ASCD Quick Reference Guide *Principles and Practices for Effective Blended Learning* (with Eric Carbaugh) and *Smart in the Middle Grades: Classrooms That Work for Bright Middle Schoolers* (with Carol Ann Tomlinson). Kristina's current research focuses on standards-based grading, integrated ELA instruction, and innovative instruction for English language learners. She taught middle and high school language arts for 10 years and has served as an instructional coach and curriculum developer in elementary and middle school classrooms for an additional 20 years.

Kristina can be reached at kjdoubet@mac.com, www.KristinaDoubet.com, and on Twitter @kjdoubet.

Related ASCD Resources: Collaborative Learning and Differentiated Instruction

At the time of publication, the following resources were available (ASCD stock numbers in parentheses):

The Best Class You Never Taught: How Spider Web Discussion Can Turn Students into Learning Leaders by Alexis Wiggins (#117017)

Demystifying Discussions: How to Teach and Assess Academic Conversation Skills, K–5 by Jennifer Orr (#122003)

Differentiation in the Elementary Grades: Strategies to Engage and Equip All Learners by Kristina J. Doubet and Jessica A. Hockett (#117014)

Differentiation in Middle and High Schools: Strategies to Engage All Learners by Kristina J. Doubet and Jessica A. Hockett (#115008)

Grading and Group Work: How do I assess individual learning when students work together? (ASCD Arias) by Susan M. Brookhart (#SF113073)

How to Differentiate Instruction in Academically Diverse Classrooms, 3rd Edition by Carol Ann Tomlinson (#117032)

Improving Student Collaboration with Flexible Grouping (Quick Reference Guide) by Kristina J. Doubet (#QRG121012)

Questioning for Classroom Discussion: Purposeful Speaking, Engaged Listening, Deep Thinking by Jackie Acree Walsh and Beth Dankert Sattes (#115012)

Student Learning Communities: A Springboard for Academic and Social-Emotional Development by Douglas Fisher, Nancy Frey, and John Almarode (#121030)

Understanding Differentiated Instruction (Quick Reference Guide) by Carol Ann Tomlinson (#QRG117094)

For up-to-date information about ASCD resources, go to www.ascd.org. You can search the complete archives of *Educational Leadership* at www.ascd.org/el.

For more information, send an email to member@ascd.org; call 1-800-933-2723 or 703-578-9600; send a fax to 703-575-5400; or write to Information Services, ASCD, 1703 N. Beauregard St., Alexandria, VA 22311-1714 USA.

WHOLE CHILD
TENETS

 1 HEALTHY
Each student enters school healthy and learns about and practices a healthy lifestyle.

2 SAFE
Each student learns in an environment that is physically and emotionally safe for students and adults.

 3 ENGAGED
Each student is actively engaged in learning and is connected to the school and broader community.

The ASCD Whole Child approach is an effort to transition from a focus on narrowly defined academic achievement to one that promotes the long-term development and success of all children. Through this approach, ASCD supports educators, families, community members, and policymakers as they move from a vision about educating the whole child to sustainable, collaborative actions.

4 SUPPORTED
Each student has access to personalized learning and is supported by qualified, caring adults.

The Flexibly Grouped Classroom relates to the **safe**, **engaged**, **supported**, and **challenged** tenets.

For more about the ASCD Whole Child approach, visit **www. ascd.org/wholechild.**

 5 CHALLENGED
Each student is challenged academically and prepared for success in college or further study and for employment and participation in a global environment.